Shakespeare's Stories: **The Tragedies**
Retold by Beverley Birch

"True to the power and poetry of the original plays, these dramatic retellings, illustrated with occasional small drawings, will help attract the reluctant and the intimidated to the pleasure of Shakespeare."

—Booklist

"Birch spellbinds her reader for she retains so much of Shakespeare's original characterization, tone, and important quotations. Highly recommended."

—Fairfax, VA. Media Services

"In clear direct prose, Ms. Birch has captured the power and humor of the original plays. She has retained the flavor of the plays with the use of Shakespeare's own language in major scenes. Black-and-white illustrations sustain the reader's interest in the stories."

—Educational Media & Technology Services, Charlotte, NC.

"The artwork is extraordinary; the details add much to the textual material; the emotions of the characters in these plays are fully drawn. A must-have. . . ."

—Meadowcreek Learning Resource Center, Ft. Worth, TX.

"Birch has done an excellent job of retelling Shakespeare's plays in story form. . . . Highly recommended."

—The Book Report

SHAKESPEARE'S STORIES
Tragedies

Retold by Beverley Birch

Illustrated by Tony Kerins

PETER BEDRICK BOOKS

NEW YORK

First American edition published in 1988 by
Peter Bedrick Books, New York

Text copyright © 1988 Beverley Birch
Illustrations copyright © Macdonald & Co. (Publishers) Ltd.

Published by agreement with Macdonald & Co. (Publishers) Ltd., London.
A member of Pergamon MCC Publishing Corporation plc.

Library of Congress Cataloging-in-Publication Data
Birch, Beverley.
    Shakespeare's stories: tragedies/retold by Beverley Birch;
Illustrated by Tony Kerins. – 1st American ed.
      p. cm.
    Contents: King Lear – Othello – Hamlet – Macbeth – Romeo and Juliet.
    ISBN 0–87226–193–X
    ISBN 0–87226–227–8 (pbk.)
    1. Shakespeare, William, 1564–1616 – Adaptations – Juvenile
literature. 2. Shakespeare, William, 1564–1616 – Tragedies – Juvenile
literature. [1. Shakespeare, William, 1564–1616 – Adaptations.
2. Shakespeare, William, 1564–1616 – Tragedies.] I. Shakespeare,
William, 1564–1616.   II. Kerins, Tony, ill. III. Title.
PR2877.B46 1988
813'.54dc19
                                          88–18112
                                             CIP
                                             AC

Printed in Great Britain
10 9 8 7 6 5 4 3 2
First paperback edition 1990

The author's grateful thanks are due to Priscilla Stone for her perceptive
comment, criticism and never-flagging encouragement, and to Ruairidh
and Calum MacLean, who have tirelessly read the scripts with the
healthy scepticism of a young eye, and whose comments have been a
source of inspiration and much-valued guidance.

-CONTENTS-

Macbeth

Sunless mists turned about the place, and rocks crouched low beneath a rumbling thunder. Into the circle of the gloom they came, twisting figures woven in the air; and with them came dark whisperings:

'When shall we three meet again, in thunder, lightning or in rain?'
Hoarse with a poisonous hate, the answer lingered.
'When the hurlyburly's done; when the battle's lost . . . and won.'
The sodden earth began to tremble . . .
'That will be before the set of sun.'
'Where the place?'
'Upon the heath.' A curdling wail rose through the air, as though a thousand wretched creatures were imprisoned in that moaning place.

'There to meet with *Macbeth*!' The final venomous shriek swept from the writhing shadows low across the heather and then up, up into the eye of a blackly gathering storm . . .

King Duncan's camp was bright and quick with movement. Men strode fast between low flickering fires and every hour the messengers sped from the battlefield towards the waiting king.

A soldier stumbled into camp, staggered, and fell. They saw the staring horror of a long-fought battle in his face and ropes of blood draining his filth-streaked limbs.

They raised him up and sent for dressings for the wounds, while battle-weary men gathered around.

Between hoarse, panting breaths the soldier spilled his tale: how bitterly the battle ebbed and flowed! Neither the soldiers of the king nor those of the rebel army were gaining ground, until . . . his voice broke, sobbed, and listeners drew closer, fearing the worst. It seemed the villainous rebel Macdonwald gained a hold and viciously pressed forward his attack! And then . . . .

'Brave Macbeth! Well he deserves that name!' the soldier cried, and a new fire coursed through his limbs, as with his arms swung wide he showed the mighty swordsweeps of Macbeth. His listeners could almost see Macbeth carve his unflinching path through spear and axe.

'At last,' he said, 'Macbeth stood face to face against Macdonwald.' And now the soldier stood erect, as though he would draw Macbeth's great strength into his own battered limbs. And with gigantic swirling blows he showed how Macbeth battled Macdonwald towards his death. A mighty, final deathstroke the soldier gave and there before the watchers' eyes, the rebel Macdonwald fell.

'O valiant cousin!' King Duncan's voice shook. How could his gratitude for Macbeth's valour be weighed in words? It seemed that Scotland's fate, the people's lives, his own, were cradled in the vast courage of this warrior's breast.

'But mark, King of Scotland, mark,' the soldier swayed and a grey weariness drained his face. 'The King of Norway with new supplies of men began a fresh assault!'

'Did this dismay our generals, Macbeth and Banquo?' the King questioned urgently.

'Yes . . .' A sharp in-drawn breath hissed through the crowd. So the battle was now lost! The soldier drew up his trembling body and threw his shoulders wide. 'As sparrows would dismay the eagle or the hare dismay the lion!'

'Ah . . .' the single murmur of relief swept around, with nods and smiles. Even now they could see Macbeth and Banquo, fighting stroke for stroke against the enemy, their demon onslaught drawing other soldiers on with new-born strength! But now the soldier who told the tale grew faint, and sank to the ground.

'Your wounds tell of your honour, as do your words,' King Duncan said. 'Go, get him to the surgeons.'

He swung suddenly on his heel as a new commotion sounded at the gate. It was the Thane of Ross, hot-foot from the battlefield. He sped through the camp towards them. 'God save the King!' he cried. 'The King of Norway himself, helped by that disloyal traitor the Thane of Cawdor, began a dismal conflict! Until our general, Macbeth, like the unvanquished God of War, confronted him sword point against point, arm against arm . . .' The thane's voice soared with triumph, 'and, to conclude, the victory fell on us!'

'Great happiness!' King Duncan's voice broke. He raised his arms silently, as though to encircle every loyal man. The bloody course of battle was now run and all the rebels were in flight. His aged shoulders straightened, as though finally he threw off a weighty burden. What rich rewards were owed by him to loyal men! He sighed: so too was punishment owed to the rebel lord who joined with an invading king.

Swiftly he gave commands. Traitors would no more betray this land: *death* would be the payment for that Thane of Cawdor's treachery.

'And with the traitor's title,' triumphantly the king announced, 'greet Macbeth.' His voice grew sombre. 'What Cawdor has lost, noble Macbeth has won!' With these words King Duncan's hand rose up, slowly, as though the great Macbeth were cradled in his royal grasp.

Storm clouds swelled above the heath. The last rim of light lingered, hopelessly, and then was smothered.

At the crossroads, the air grew heavy. Gorsebushes and blackened tree stumps trembled. Darkness sank, thick and dark and oily; and from its centre a reeking vapour coiled, snaked upward from the earth, spiralled and spread . . .

Within, three figures moved: twisted forms of wizened skin and knotted hair. Locked one to the other in a grimly rhythmic sway they turned, now this way, now the other, the murmur of their chant like some fiendish heartbeat in the rising howl of winds.

Above the gale a drumbeat boomed. The figures paused, and swivelled towards the sound and a glow of ugly glee enflamed their watching faces.

Macbeth and Banquo trod a weary path across the heath, and with resounding drumbeat Banquo killed the memories of horror on the field of war.

Macbeth walked deep in thought. He shrugged his shoulders high against the winds.

Banquo's drumbeat stopped. Into their faces rose a stench as though a rottenness steamed from the caverns of a poisonous earth. Three withered forms rose to their gaze: gnarled skeletons of rag and bone sheathed in a bloody light. Each raised a crooked finger to skinny lips.

Macbeth shivered. An iciness seeped through his bones.

He summoned all his will.

'Speak if you can! What are you?' His command rose into the wind.

One grisly figure rasped a crackling chant:

'All hail Macbeth! hail to thee, Thane of Glamis!'

Another, 'all hail, Macbeth! hail to thee, Thane of Cawdor!'

The words hung in the rancid air. In that moment, waiting, Macbeth felt a coiling in his stomach, as though a serpent writhed . . .

'All hail, Macbeth! that shalt be king hereafter!'

In the warrior's heart there was a hammering as though his ribs would break. King!

To be king!

Banquo moved towards the apparitions. 'If you can look into the seeds of time, and say which grain will grow, and which will not, speak then to me . . .'

'Hail!' the creaking voices rose to a crescendo.

'Lesser than Macbeth, and greater.'

'Not so happy, yet much happier.'

'Thou shalt get kings, though thou be none!'

Macbeth broke across their rhythm. 'Tell me more: I know I am Thane of Glamis; but how of Cawdor? The Thane of Cawdor lives . . .' he paused, 'and to be king . . .' It was beyond belief. How could they know? What more might they foresee?

'Speak!' he cried, more urgently, but already the gory glow that held the monstrous trio began to seep into the sodden ground; their forms began to melt. Only the odour of decay hung in the leaden air.

Macbeth and Banquo were alone again.

'Your children shall be kings,' murmured Macbeth.

'*You* shall be king,' Banquo's voice betrayed the wonder of his half-belief.

Macbeth's thoughts churned. There *is* a king: There *is* a Thane of Cawdor. The storm shrieked the words into a thundering pattern inside his head.

'Who's here?' At Banquo's sudden cry, two men broke through the gloom towards them, breathless with the burden of their news: the fame of Macbeth's battle deeds had reached the king and they now brought the monarch's thanks to him.

And yet their words were almost lost, for he was hearing other voices in the wind. Until the words '*the Thane of Cawdor*' pierced his thoughts: the Thane of Cawdor had been judged a traitor, and as thanks for Macbeth's services in war, and sign of honours yet to come, the king *now gave Macbeth that name.*

The prophecy! Already one part true.

What of the other part? Before his eyes there rose an image of the king. Bold, strong, alive.

Yet *I* should be king. The hammering in his ribs grew stronger. Hair rose across his scalp, as though some dreadful thought was searching for a nesting place within his brain.

And yet, the image was already there.

The vision of a single, bloody act.

To kill the king.

The thought swelled, and became alive, and Macbeth struggled to push it back.

'Come friends,' he forced himself to say, 'let us towards the king . . .'

In the palace the king awaited news. Had Cawdor been executed yet? The business troubled him.

'He was a gentleman on whom I built an absolute trust,' he murmured to Malcolm, his son. He sighed: how little of what a person really thought was written on their face! He grew weary with this sorrow; his trust had been so painfully misplaced.

There was a sudden commotion in the Court and cries of jubilant welcome. Macbeth and Banquo had come! The king rose swiftly to meet them: such true men they were, throwing their lives behind their loyalty to Scotland and her king!

'O worthiest cousin!' his heart overflowed with all he owed Macbeth: more, more than ever he could pay.

Macbeth stood, great and battle-stained before his king.

'Our duties,' he paused, beating back a thousand whirling thoughts, 'our duties are to your throne and state. We do only what we should, by doing everything to ensure your safety, love and honour.'

For a long, silent moment, the king grasped his hand. 'Welcome! You are welcome here!'

And now he turned to Macbeth's staunch companion.

'Noble Banquo! You have deserved no less.' Warmly he embraced his general, and turned away to wipe the joyful tears which now flowed freely down his cheeks.

Then he swung with sudden resolution to face the waiting Court. 'Sons, kinsmen, thanes,' he said, steadying his voice, 'know that I now declare as heir to my throne and state . . .'

Macbeth looked up, a quickening pulse beating below his temple. So soon! The final prophecy!

And yet the king was moving past him and placing a hand upon the shoulder of his son!

' . . . my eldest, Malcolm. We name him heir to the throne and Prince of Cumberland.'

A mist of whispering thoughts leapt to Macbeth's brain. He was not to be the future king, but the king's son Malcolm, would be instead!

That is a step, he breathed, on which I must fall down, or else . . . he searched for his answer, and a restless anguish coiled within him: the serpent of ambition writhed – he recognized it fully now. He saw the crown on Duncan's head burning as a beacon to draw him on. He *would* be king.

'Stars, hide your fires. Let not light see my black and deep desires.'

The lady lifted the letter to the flickering light and read again. A strange tale, her lord Macbeth told her! Bewitched encounters on the heath; glorious honours foretold. The letter breathed fire into her very limbs, and answered an inward flame.

She seemed to see her husband stand before her, tall and strong.

'Glamis you are, and Cawdor,' she murmured, 'and you shall be what you are promised.'

And yet, she saw him too, too clearly. 'I do fear your nature. It is too full of the milk of human kindness.' How well she knew that! He wanted greatness, power, wealth; but would not willingly play falsely for it. He yearned for that which was not his; and yet he would not do what *must* be done, to win.

'Macbeth,' she longed to see him. 'Hurry to me, that I may pour my courage in your ear . . .' There was a sudden movement at the door. A messenger! She turned urgently to hear his news.

'The king comes here tonight,' he said.

'Tonight!' She signalled him away and turned, to gaze far into the distance beyond the castle walls.

Tonight! She closed her eyes. Deep within her lungs, her stomach, her loins, she drew breath, as though she would suck the fires from the centre of the earth.

'Come you spirits that wait on human thoughts,' she cried, 'fill me

11

from crown to toe top-full of direst cruelty! Make thick my blood . . .
come, come, thick night . . .'

Tonight they would begin the climb towards the crown. Tonight they
would kill the king. She saw the crown now, shining only for them . . .
It was there Macbeth found her, and wordlessly they clung together.

'My dearest love,' he murmured then, not looking in her eyes,
'Duncan comes here tonight,' and he turned restlessly to avoid her
searching gaze.

She seized his face and swung it towards her, and her hand was steel.
'You shall put this night's business into *my* care.'

Hastily Macbeth drew back from her, lowering his eyes. 'We will
speak further.'

'Only look up!' she urged. 'Leave all the rest to me!'

The royal party came at dusk: the king and his two sons, Malcolm and
Donalbain; Banquo and all the noble lords. Their mood was light. The
fruits of victory against the enemy were now secured, and it gave to all
of them a pleasant lack of care. They marvelled at the sweet summer air
that flowed so softly about Macbeth's castle. And how warmly did his
lady welcome them into her home! Words of honour and loving debt
flowed from her lips, and in the evening she prepared a sumptuous
banquet for her royal guests.

It pleased King Duncan well. The castle halls rang with the joyful
sound of music; servants flew to and fro; great dishes steamed with the
rich odours of succulent foods and torches flamed a merry welcome.

Only Macbeth left the festivities, suddenly, and sought the dark.
Alone in the courtyard, he strode to and fro.

What visions bedevilled his tired brain! If only such deeds as he
imagined could be swiftly done, and ended there. But could there ever
be rest again after the murder of a king? Could there ever be sleep again
after the killing of a man so gracious, noble, kind, as Duncan?

'He's here in double trust,' he told himself. 'First, as I am his cousin
and his subject; and then, as I am his host, who should shut the door
against his murderer, not bear the knife myself!'

And yet the serpent coiled within him still. To be king! To rule all
Scotland!

Lady Macbeth came searching for him, angrily.

'We'll go no further in this business,' he said to her.

12

Such scorn she spat at him and he winced beneath its lash!

'Are you afraid?'

'Peace,' Macbeth struggled against her rage. 'I dare do all that is fitting for a man.'

'What beast was it then, that made you break this enterprise to me? When you *dared* do it, *then* you were a man!'

He strove to find another reason against the deed: 'If we should fail?'

'We fail! But screw your courage to the sticking place and we'll not fail!' She stood before him, certain in her power. And step by step, she laid her deadly plan before him: Duncan's servant would be overpowered with wine and fall into a drunken stupor. 'What cannot you and I perform upon the unguarded Duncan then?'

Her certainties lulled him. The bloody visions stilled.

It was all settled, now.

They stood together, each with their private vision of the golden promises to come. Each bone and sinew must be steeled and bent to do this horrible thing. Macbeth prepared.

He waited, shrouded in the darkness of the court. The revelry was over and all the guests were in bed; Macbeth alone listened for the bell to call him to the night's grim task.

How long those minutes were until that dread bell's note!

He looked into the shadows, moving with an uneasy tread. And then he halted, staring, aghast.

'Is this a dagger which I see before me, the handle towards my hand?' He tried to seize the weapon, but his fingers passed through air. And still the blade hung there!

And now it dripped with blood!

He stumbled back against the stair that led towards the king.

'There's no such thing,' he cried. 'It is this bloody business which brings it to my eyes!'

Against the wall, he felt the hardness of the stone along his back. This wall was real. So was the earth on which he stood. He braced himself and stilled his trembling mind.

The bell! Far off it tolled. The summons from his wife coursed through his body like a fire, and drew him on, on up the stair, towards the sleeping king . . .

His wife came into the blanketing gloom within the court. She had drunk some of the wine that she had given to King Duncan's guards and it had fired her inward flame.

She was now ready.

She strained her ears towards the rooms beyond the stairs.

'He is about it.'

She listened again. 'I laid their daggers ready; he could not miss them!' But what if the guards awoke before Macbeth had killed the king? She raised her hands against her face. They trembled, and she had not known they would.

She thought then of the king, asleep, at peace, as she had seen him only a few moments ago, and a sudden ache stirred through her. 'Had he not looked like my father as he slept, I would have done it.'

A shuffling lurch came on the stair above! Macbeth swayed there, ashen-faced.

'I have done the deed,' he whispered. 'Did you not hear a noise?'

'I heard the owl scream and the crickets cry,' she answered him. 'Did *you* not speak?'

'When?'

'Now.'

'As I descended?' he searched the darkness beyond her.

'Ay,' she moved towards him.

He pulled away and stared at his bloody hands. 'This is a sorry sight.'

'A foolish thought to say a sorry sight!' she retorted angrily.

He raised his eyes and looked into her face, and what eyes they were! And then he froze, as though somewhere within the winds that gathered round their towers he'd heard a sound. He pointed a trembling finger, 'I thought I heard a voice cry "sleep no more, Macbeth has murdered sleep."'

'What do you mean?' she cried.

He stumbled to the window, 'Still it cried "Sleep no more! . . . Glamis has murdered sleep, and therefore Cawdor shall sleep no more; Macbeth shall sleep no more!"'

She seized his arm, and she was scornful now.

'Go, get some water and wash this filthy witness from your hand.' In horror she seized the blades clutched in his fingers. 'Why did you bring these daggers from the place? They must lie there: go carry them.'

'I'll go no more!' Macbeth gasped, hoarse, 'I am afraid to think what I have done. Look on it again, I dare not.'

'Give me the daggers!' She sped up the stairs. And if the king was bleeding, why she would smear his blood across the guards and everyone would see that it was *they* who had done this thing!

A thunderous knocking boomed across the court. Macbeth shuddered, and did not move.

'What hands are here? They pluck out my eyes! All great Neptune's ocean will not wash this blood clean from my hand!'

She had returned, and now her hands too reeked with Duncan's blood! He recoiled in horror as she held them up. 'My hands are of your colour, but I shame to wear a heart so white!' she said.

Again the knocking thundered. She urged his attention, pulling him towards their rooms. 'A little water clears us of this deed. How easy it is then!' The knocking came again. 'Hark! Get on your nightgown.'

As though he saw the hammer of doom beyond, Macbeth stared wretchedly at the outer door. 'Wake Duncan with this knocking! I wish you could!'

It was Macduff, the noble Thane of Fife who came with other lords to wake the king. They hammered at the castle door and shivered in the bitter morning chill. How warm the summer bloom of evening air had been the night before; and yet what storms had torn the sky since then! The wind had seemed to scream with agony, and trembling, like a fever, shook the earth.

Macbeth greeted them, dressed in his nightgown and told them the king was not yet up.

'I'll bring you to him,' Macbeth said.

He led Macduff towards the room. The thane went in. There was a moment as he crossed the floor, a pause, a strangled gasp, and then a cry that pierced the very stones around them.

'O horror, horror, horror! Awake, awake!' Macduff's voice rang throughout the castle. 'Murder and treason! Banquo and Donalbain! Malcolm! Awake!'

Bells rang, torches flamed and the castle echoed with running feet.

Lady Macbeth hurried to them: what hideous thing had so alarmed her guests?

'Our royal master's murdered!'

Who? Who had done it? His guards! Bathed in the king's blood, confused and babbling, their filthy daggers lying on their pillows . . .

But Macbeth, in fury for the murder of his king, it seemed, had taken swift revenge and killed them instantly!

'Why did you do so?' Macduff exclaimed. It startled him. So swiftly to kill those they could question about the night's unnatural events: their punishment was too hastily done!

Or was it? A grain was seeded in Macduff's mind, even as he heard the words of grief spilling from Macbeth's lips. He watched him. And Lady Macbeth watched Macduff.

Could this bold thane already see the lies that lurked below the surface of her husband's words? Did he suspect Macbeth had killed the guards to stop them talking?

'Help me!' she swayed, as though about to faint.

'Look to the lady,' Macduff commanded. They rushed to help her. And no one else, it seemed, had seen what he had seen.

Within the hour Malcolm and Donalbain sped from the castle. It seemed to Malcolm that the murderer of a king would turn next to the murder of the sons and heirs to that king's throne. Here, for them, there were daggers in men's smiles.

The dark spirits of the heath had sowed their poisonous seed and what rich soil it had found! How it had grown and fruited!

And now the crop was nearly in: King Duncan dead and Malcolm, the heir to the throne, in flight. It seemed to everyone that it must prove his guilt: he must have bribed the guards to murder his own father.

The nobles sought a new heir to the throne of Scotland. Macbeth! So loyal and honest a cousin to king Duncan; and had he not in battle proved his love for Scotland and her king?

And so Macbeth took up the crown, and no one could deny so worthy a man ascending to Duncan's royal seat.

Except Macduff, the noble Thane of Fife. He did not attend the coronation of Macbeth, but watched it from afar, and wondered.

Banquo remained, adviser to Macbeth. But such cursed thoughts he'd had since that dark day upon the heath, and such vile dreams now mocked his sleep!

He thought of the new-made king, Macbeth. 'You have it now,' he murmured. 'King, Cawdor, Glamis, all as the weird women promised, and I fear you played most foully for it.'

But had they not also said that he would be root and father of many kings? The promise beckoned him, and yet his nature struggled with the poison of the witches' words, and deep within, he knew how Macbeth had taken the crown . . .

Macbeth came to him, richly dressed in royal robes and attended by his queen, the lords and nobles of the Court. He announced, 'Tonight, we hold a ceremonial supper, sir, and I request your presence.'

'Let your highness command me,' Banquo replied. Each minute his distance from this man who was his friend seemed to get wider.

'Will you ride this afternoon?' Macbeth enquired. 'Is it far you ride?'

'As far, my lord, as will fill up the time between now and supper.'

The king nodded, thoughtfully. 'Fail not our feast.' And he watched Banquo go, taking his young son with him. This man now woke a fear in Macbeth's breast that clawed deep as a dagger's blade.

'There is no one but he whose being I do fear,' he thought. Brave, wise Banquo: he knew of the dark women on the heath, and of their promises. And had they not hailed him as father to a line of kings? 'To *me* they did not speak of heirs: no son will follow *me* onto the throne.'

The barren prospect chilled Macbeth with a new and terrifying pain. To have dredged up such evil from within his soul; to have stilled all the warmth of loyalty, honour, love, humanity! And all for what?

'Then I have defiled my mind for Banquo's sons. For them I have murdered the gracious Duncan. For Banquo's heirs I have given up my soul to the dark spirits and surrendered sleep to the shuddering visions of these endless nights . . .'

The agony worked deep within him, bending him towards new avenues of hate. He sent for cloaked, hidden men with scowling desperation on their faces. And in their hands Macbeth now laid the lives of Banquo and his son. This threat to him *would* end; snuffed like a candle even as they rode towards his feast.

And all the while the queen roamed listlessly. A drugging weariness now bedevilled every step she took. All had seemed so simple when she planned it: the crown was so near at hand, so easy for the taking, and the murder of a man so quick, so neatly done.

And yet what was it worth, now that they had it all?

'My lord, why do you keep alone?', she questioned Macbeth again. She ached to stand with him as once she had, when that shining thread of their ambition had woven them together. 'What's done is done,' she pleaded, but her words fell on stony ground.

'We have scorched the snake, not killed it,' he retorted sharply. Could she not see the snake would return to rip his nights with poisoned tooth?

These dreams that nightly tortured him!

'So full of scorpions is my mind, dear wife!' he said to her.

'Gentle my love,' she tried to touch his face. 'Be bright and jovial among your guests tonight.'

In a dark place near the palace Macbeth's murderers did their swift butcher's work and sliced the life from Banquo. But Banquo's son escaped and fled into the night.

In the palace the ceremonial feast was laid: a royal banquet to hail a new-crowned king. Macbeth played monarch with gracious words, welcoming his guests and preparing to drink a toast to them.

There was a sudden movement. The murderer came to the door with blood smeared on his face, and hastily Macbeth went to him. Was Banquo dead? Yes, his throat was cut, and twenty deep gashes on his head. His son? His son had fled!

The fear swelled in him like the last wave that would drown him as he stood. He braced himself, and turned towards the celebration feast, summoning the smilings of a host onto his face. The lords hailed him to sit with them.

'The table's full,' he said. He could not see an empty place to sit. Even where they showed him there was a place, there was a man . . .

But it was not a man! It was the tatters of a man, all gashed and soaked with blood, his head half-hanging from his gaping neck . . . it stared at him, and stared . . . Macbeth cried out, 'You cannot say I did it. Never shake your gory locks at me!'

The nobles leapt in consternation to their feet; the queen urged them to sit again.

'Shame!' she hissed at trembling Macbeth. 'Why do you make such faces? When all's done, you look but on a stool!' He looked, and it was gone. He straightened up and breathed again.

'The time has been that, when the brains were out, the man would die, and there an end,' he assured the startled Court. 'But now they rise again and push us from our stools!'

The queen seized his arm. Had he lost all his sense? The nobles would hear and know what they had done! She urged him towards the feast. He strained to hold his mind and body firm, and once more he approached the table.

Again! Banquo! All pale and bloody, and staring with sightless eyes!

He tried to shield himself, 'How can you behold such sights,' he accused the watching nobles, 'and keep the natural ruby of your cheeks when mine are blanched with fear?'

'What sights, my lord?' a thane enquired of him.

'I pray you, speak not,' the queen pleaded. 'He is not well. Question enrages him. Stand not upon the order of your going, but go at once!'

They went. But they had heard.

'It will have blood,' Macbeth murmured wretchedly. 'They say blood will have blood.'

His wife stood watching him. There was no life left in her now. All was spent. She saw how far beyond her reach he now had moved! Sleep beckoned her, only sleep. How long was it since she, or he, had slept?

Macbeth's brain fastened on a new thought. Macduff! He had not come to celebrate. Macduff *refused* to celebrate his kingship! Macbeth knew, for did he not keep spies in every noble's court? Did he not need them to sniff out the hidden treacheries that rose against a king!

Fears pressed down on him from every side and hemmed him in. Suddenly he made up his mind. 'I will tomorrow, early, go to the weird sisters. More shall they speak, for now I am bent to know, by the worst means, the worst. For my own good, all others shall give way! I wade so deep in blood already that returning would be as wretched as going on!'

Now the strange behaviour of the king was known, and far and wide the people talked of it. They said that he was mad, and whispered of the bloody path by which he had mounted to the throne.

It was also known that Malcolm had received a royal welcome in England, at King Edward's court. There also Macduff, the Thane of Fife, had gone, to ask the English king for help. He said that Malcolm the rightful heir to Duncan, should come against Macbeth, the murdering usurper of the royal throne of Scotland.

Macbeth learned of these moves against him, and prepared.

He found the twisted women of the heath in a deep cavern, brooding like vultures above a cauldron's stream. They swayed and moaned and threw some vile, rotting thing into the bilious brew, and grimly their chant rose above the cauldron's hiss.

'Round about the cauldron go
In the poisoned entrails throw.

Double, double toil and trouble;
Fire burn and cauldron bubble.

Fillet of a fenny snake.
In the cauldron boil and bake;
Eye of newt and toe of frog,
Wool of bat and tongue of dog . . .

Double, double toil and trouble;
Fire burn and cauldron bubble.'

'How now, you secret, black and midnight hags!' he cried. 'I conjure you, answer me!'

To his command there came a crash of thunder. From the cauldron rose a helmeted head which opened bloodless lips and spoke:

'Macbeth! Macbeth! Beware Macduff. Beware the Thane of Fife!'

The vision sank. His fears were real! Thunder rolled again, and now an infant hovered above the cauldron's stench, its body and its tiny limbs all stained with blood as though new born. It spoke!

'Be bloody, bold and resolute; laugh to scorn the power of man, for none of woman born shall harm Macbeth.'

His heart surged with new hope. 'Then live, Macduff: Why need I fear you? You had a mother who gave birth to you, as do we all . . .' And yet . . . he would kill him, just to be sure, just to strangle these swarming terrors.

Thunder again: the image of a child that wore a crown and held a branch towards him.

'Be lion-mettled, proud,' the vision spoke. 'Macbeth shall never vanquished be until great Birnam Wood to high Dunsinane Hill shall come against him.'

His courage soared. Safe! Safe! How could a wood take up its roots and move? The rebellion raised against him in England could never

win. Not until the wood at Birnam moved! He laughed to think of it.

'Yet my heart throbs to know one thing,' he questioned urgently. 'Shall Banquo's descendants ever reign in this kingdom?'

The cauldron sank into the ground, and now there came a line of kings: one, two, three, . . . each one with Banquo's face, and the vision burned his eyes out, for their crowns shone like the sun itself . . . six, seven, and in a mirror the eighth one showed him a score of others gliding after . . . And all the while the bloody Banquo smiled and smiled and showed they were all his!

Macbeth fell to his knees, covering his face. All this vast sea of evil he had steeped his being in, and yet it would be Banquo's descendants on the throne, not his . . .

Round about the fallen figure the withered women danced.

Suddenly he was alone. He stumbled to his feet. Gone? 'Damned be all those that trust them,' he cried.

There seemed no end to Scotland's wounds. The country sank beneath the yoke of an enraged and corrupted king: it wept, it bled, and each new day a gash was added to the festering wounds. His villainies seemed to taint the very air that Scotland's people breathed.

At first, Macbeth plotted Macduff's death. But then he learned Macduff had reached England, and as if no evil was now beyond his fevered grasp, he ordered instead the deaths of all who could be found inside the castle of Macduff! The children, wife, the servants of the Thane of Fife – all put to the knife by Macbeth's murderers.

But good men began to gather against his tyranny. Macbeth went to the great castle at high Dunsinane to prepare for war, and with him went the queen.

But she was no longer like the queen. She was a shadow, pale and lifeless, except when she walked by night, asleep.

Her gentlewoman fetched the doctor to see what illness could so shake the queen that she would leave her bed and wander in the echoing halls, would make her always keep a candle by her side as though she shrank from some dark menace in the night.

They waited secretly for her. There came the flicker of her candle, and the wasted figure of the queen moved into sight. She walked as in a trance, rubbing her thin white hands as though she washed them, but with such violence as if she tried to rip the skin from every bone.

'Yet here's a spot,' she gasped. 'Out, out, damned spot! Out I say!' She shuddered: but she could see the blood was on them still!

She thought she saw her husband stand before her now, as once he was. 'Fie, my lord, fie! A soldier, and afraid! What need we fear who knows it?' She searched the dark, and sobbed, 'Who would have thought the old man to have had so much blood in him?' And she half sang, 'The Thane of Fife had a wife. Where is she now?'

Her trembling hands rose before her face.

'What, will these hands never be clean? Here's the smell of blood still.' And with a long, piteous sigh, she sobbed, 'All the perfumes of Arabia will not sweeten this little hand.'

Suddenly she stood tall and shook her head reproachfully.

'Wash your hands, put on your nightgown. Look not so pale. I tell you yet again Banquo's buried; he cannot come out of his grave.'

The listeners heard, aghast. Now the source of madness in the queen, was clear!

'Look after her,' the doctor urged. 'Remove from her the means of all harm to herself and always keep your eyes on her.'

Not far from Dunsinane the Scottish lords were gathering, and even men close to Macbeth now went to lend their strength to Malcolm's cause. They prepared to meet the English force with Malcolm and Macduff near Birnam Wood.

Macbeth fortified Dunsinane. But what need he fear these armies massing against him? Could Birnam Wood ever move to Dunsinane? 'Never! Macduff was born of woman; no man born of woman shall ever have power over me, so said the women of the heath!'

But still there was no rest for him. He reeled with tiredness and an inward, festering wound that turned all sour.

'I'll fight,' he cried, with sudden, savage rage. 'I'll fight till from my bones my flesh be hacked. Give me my armour!'

'It is not needed yet,' they told him.

'I'll put it on! Send out more horses; scour the country round; hang all those that talk of fear! Give me my armour!' And then he flung the servant from him. 'Pull it off, I say!'

The English and the Scottish armies met at Birnam Wood. Malcolm surveyed the host of men joined with him against the tyrant and he was proud. 'Let every soldier cut down a branch and bear it before him,' he commanded. 'So shall we hide our numbers from Macbeth.'

Within the castle Macbeth gave commands. 'Hang out our banners on the outward walls.'

A sudden cry came from the inner rooms, a wail so stark, and desolate and chill it should have iced him to his heart. But what was one more desolation, one more horror to him now?

His servant brought the news.

'The queen, my Lord, is dead.'

Macbeth turned away. What a vacant, futile life this was, when all was done. The future and the past yawned with arid emptiness on either side of him.

'Tomorrow and tomorrow and tomorrow creep in this petty pace from day to day to the last syllable of recorded time.' He searched for the purpose in it, but there was none. 'Life's but a tale told by an idiot, full of sound and fury, signifying *nothing* . . .'

A messenger burst in on him. 'As I stood watch upon the hill I looked towards Birnam and I thought the wood began to move!'

A dark, ravaging terror took Macbeth. Fear not, the fiends had said, till Birnam Wood do come to Dunsinane.

And now it came.

He thrust the terror from him. 'Arm, arm and out. Ring the alarms. Blow wind, come wrack! At least we'll die with armour on our back!'

Beyond the fortress walls the drums of Malcolm's soldiers boomed and trumpets called to war. 'Throw down your leafy screens,' Malcolm commanded his men. 'Show yourselves as those you are!'

Macbeth came from the fortress, fighting, scorning all. One final prophecy was yet to come. 'The fiends have tied me to a stake,' he cried, 'I cannot fly, but like a bear I must fight the course! What's he that was not born of woman? Such a one am I to fear, or none!'

Great Dunsinane surrendered to Malcolm's force. Now Duncan's son and heir strode through the gates as victor of the day.

Macduff sought Macbeth everywhere. He blistered for the lives of all his murdered children, wife, and all. He burned for Scotland's wrongs.

'Turn, hell-hound, turn!' he cried.

Macbeth turned, and faced the great Macduff: traitor against royal thane. A full circle the wheel had come, since he, Macbeth, loyal thane, had faced the traitors once. It seemed as though all the evil of his poisonous days now menaced him in this one man.

'Get back,' he urged. 'My soul is weighed too heavily already with your blood. Get back!'

'I have no words, my voice is in my sword.' Macduff defied him, and leapt forward.

Macbeth held him at bay. 'I bear a charmed life,' he panted, 'which must not yield to one of woman born.'

'Then despair,' Macduff cried, 'and let the demons that have guided you tell you that I, Macduff, was ripped from my mother's womb before my time!'

So, the last twisted fruit of bitter evil was now plucked. How they had played with him, those sisters of the heath, with double talk and circling promises that lead him ever on towards false hope! And how he had fed and nurtured their poison.

But he had reached the end. And as if to redeem the broken promise of his once glorious life, he surged towards Macduff; as though by fighting he would again draw through his veins all the honour, courage and warmth that once he'd had.

But Macbeth's time was done, as was his queen's. Macduff it was that

plucked his life away and drew off the poison in the land. In killing
Macbeth he gave Scotland back her rightful line of kings. And with
great Macbeth's death, tyranny was dead; the vicious flame of murder,
treachery and disorder in the land was quenched.

Macduff bowed low before Malcolm, Prince of Cumberland. 'Hail,
King of Scotland! The time is free.'

Romeo & Juliet

Within the ancient walls of fair Verona lived two families, the Capulets and the Montagues. Both, alike, were rich and honoured in the city, but both alike were poisoned by a hatred that festered deep within them. Its cause was lost long in the distant past. Only the vicious anger lingered, like the rotten odour of a crime, polluting both the families.

Capulets hated Montagues, and Montagues hated Capulets: each son and daughter, cousin, uncle, aunt, each servant, cat and dog had bred the venom deep into their veins. Twice already in the blistering heat of this high summer their quarrel boiled to vicious brawls across the narrow streets and sleepy squares. Now it flared again: two bored servants of the house of Capulet taunted two servants of the Montagues, and in a flash the swords and daggers sliced amid the snarlings of wild men, like savage animals.

A young Montague named Benvolio rushed to part the struggling men; Tybalt, a young Capulet who burned for every chance to vent his fury on a Montague, leapt out into the fray. Within minutes the street was filled with Montague fighting Capulet, while women of the city hurried children in behind closed doors and pulled the shutters down against the chopping swords. And once again Verona's citizens drew rusty weapons from retirement and ran out to part the foes who seemed to have no other aim in life except to butcher one another.

There was one of the house of Montague who did not flourish a sword that day. Young Romeo was far from that blighted scene, plunged in a moody solitude. Benvolio, still panting from his efforts as a peace-maker at the brawl, met brooding Romeo wandering across the square and joined him, anxious to discover why his cousin shunned all company.

It was not difficult to tap the cause of Romeo's ache: he longed to tell.

He pined for love! A lady, Rosaline by name, bewitched him with her beauty, but would not return his love . . .

Benvolio was quick with good advice. 'Be ruled by me,' he urged his cousin Romeo. 'Forget to think of her! Examine other beauties.'

Romeo would have none of this. He wanted to remain locked in his love-sick melancholy. Forget Rosaline? He could never forget the precious treasure of her beauty!

Old Capulet was in an affable mood. Verona's prince had dealt fairly enough with him after the brawl that afternoon. Both he and Montague were bound now, on pain of death, to keep the city's peace. And it seemed to Capulet that it should not be hard for men as old as they to try, at least. More important questions filled his mind today. A young nobleman named Paris had asked for his daughter's hand in marriage! Though his daughter, Juliet, was very young to be a bride, for she had not yet turned fourteen, there could not possibly be a better suitor than this noble man. Wealthy, handsome, well-connected (he was a relative of the prince), he was the perfect husband for a daughter.

So Capulet had given permission to young Paris to woo Juliet that very night; for Capulet was giving a ball, an annual, traditional feast to which all his friends and relatives would come.

'Go, sirrah,' he told his new servant, beaming with benevolent good-humour, 'trudge about through fair Verona; find out those persons whose names are written on this list, and say to them my house and welcome await their pleasure!'

But the servant could not read. And so it was that Romeo and Benvolio, still strolling the dusty streets together, were shown this Capulet invitation list and asked to read the names on it, the servant little guessing that he asked the favour of two Montagues.

Seeing the list of names, Benvolio saw at once a merry plot to shake cousin Romeo from his gloom. The fair Rosaline would be at the Capulet feast. So would other admired beauties of Verona. If Romeo could be persuaded to go there, he could compare the haughty Rosaline with others! He clapped his arm about his cousin's shoulders. 'I will make you think your swan a crow!' he assured him confidently.

Half-enticed by this daring proposition, Romeo agreed to go. But only, he warned, so he could feast his eyes on Rosaline's splendour . . .

In the Capulet household there was much fluttering of silks and ribbons, much preening, brushing, smoothing, polishing, much rushing up and down for plates piled high with delicacies, and much cursing of the Nurse who kept disappearing with the pantry keys.

Juliet soared with anticipation of the feast's delights. What more excitement could there be than her own home alive with friends, ringing with merriment, a-gleam with party finery?

Her mother told her that young Paris sought her hand in marriage (a fine gentleman, so handsome, held in high esteem, a most worthy husband – her mother and her Nurse waxed lyrical on Paris' virtues) and Juliet agreed to look at him at least.

But marriage was not in Juliet's thoughts. She felt too young, too much in love with music, dance and song, to think of marriage.

Behind their comic masks and gorgeous, gaudy costumes, the young Montagues came boldly to the Capulet feast, for it was the custom of the day that uninvited guests, disguised, could swell the numbers of a ball and so enhance the joyful mystery of the occasion.

They came through streets that flickered with the firefly flames of torches and danced with the shadows of other maskers flitting to the ball. Yet Romeo was out of sorts with this light-hearted quest for merriment, and Mercutio, his dear and closest friend, worked hard to tease him from his persistent mood of gloom.

'Gentle Romeo. We *must* have you dance!' he chided him. 'You are a lover; borrow Cupid's wings and soar with them . . .'

Romeo would not be stung to lightness by such mockery, insisting that he be only a torchbearer at the ball and look on, perhaps to catch a glimpse of Rosaline.

But bubbling Mercutio, whose darting wit would never quake before the mysteries of life, only teased at them now, just as he teased Romeo.

'I see Queen Mab has been with you!' he winked and nodded knowingly. 'She is the fairies' midwife,' solemnly he explained, 'and she comes in shape no bigger than a precious jewel on the forefinger of a councillor, drawn by a team of tiny creatures across men's noses as they lie asleep. Her chariot is an empty hazelnut made by the squirrel and in this state she gallops, night by night, through lovers' brains, and then they dream of love!'

'Peace, peace, Mercutio, peace!' begged Romeo, half-laughing with him now. 'You talk of nothing . . .'

'True, I talk of dreams . . .' nodded Mercutio.

But Romeo had been having dreams of a different sort. His wistful dream of Rosaline had been pierced the night before by something more than the hopeless yearnings of unanswered love. Something more fearful beckoned him, beyond his reach, as though it warned of some grim process which would begin its march with this night's revels and would lead by a cold, haunting path, to death . . .

In the great ballroom of his house old Capulet stood smiling a genial welcome to his guests, urging them to drink and feast and the musicians to strike up a merry note for all to dance. He offered a cordial hand to the company of maskers who came to grace his ball, and Mercutio and Benvolio were swept away on the wings of gaiety. Amid the twinkling lights and gleaming floors, soft-slippered feet pranced and danced to the swish of silks and velvets. But Romeo saw nothing of this scene. He had seen a vision he had never seen before, a girl of such exquisite beauty . . .

He had seen Juliet. Across the dancing room her glow had caught him in its light and put all thought of Rosaline to instant flight. She seemed to burn with such radiance that all else receded into glowing dark: he saw nothing but her gleaming hair and shining eyes . . .

In rapt wonder he stood watching her. Dare he move closer?

Tybalt saw the young masker watch his cousin Juliet as though his eyes would never drink enough, and he became suspicious. He drew near, heard Romeo's voice enquiring of a passing servant who the stranger was, and anger shot through him with age-old viciousness.

'This by his voice should be a Montague,' he breathed. 'Fetch me a sword!' he told a servant. How dare a Montague invade a Capulet house, disguised, and sneer at their revelling!

Old Capulet saw his fiery nephew arming for some fight and hurried forward. Not at this feast! Not in this house!

'I'll not endure him,' hissed Tybalt, throwing off his uncle's hand.

'He shall be endured! *I* say he shall!' thundered Capulet. 'Am I master here, or you? You'll make a mutiny among my guests! You are an insolent youth. Be quiet, or I'll make you quiet.'

Flaming with thwarted hate, Tybalt withdrew. But he had not given up. He would still find his time to challenge this Montague who thumbed his nose at them!

Blind to the struggle being waged so near at hand, Romeo had drawn close to Juliet. Across the bobbing heads of dancers Juliet had seen the mysterious young man who seemed to glide towards her as if some witchcraft beyond his power propelled him on. The wonderment that shone even from his hidden face, touched an answering, slumbering flame in her. She looked, and she was captured.

She waited for him, enthralled. Their hands touched, shyly. There were half-humorous words exchanged which glowed with hidden meaning for the two, who had no eyes for anyone else in that enchanted room, no ears for any music now, but that which played within their own ears and eyes and hearts.

Romeo begged a kiss. Shyly, Juliet gave it. And then again, as though there was no time but this sweet moment, no place but that in which they stood together.

And then the world broke through and she was swept away in the broad encircling arms of Nurse to see her mother.

Who was she, this guest in Capulet's house? Romeo longed to know. But she was no guest, she was the only daughter of old Capulet.

Romeo's heart missed a beat. The only daughter of his father's enemy! Was he to stare at her across the chasm of hatred which split Montague from Capulet by a century of spilling blood?

Old Capulet, watching the masked Montagues prepare to leave, was far from fuelling this ancient war. He felt too filled with merry humour, for tonight young Paris had come to woo his daughter, Juliet!

Stay, he urged the Montagues, giving no sign that he knew who they were. But they set off, and Juliet, lingering to watch, sent Nurse to ask the stranger's name; and so she learned that it was Romeo, a Montague, the only son of her own family's greatest enemy.

'My only love sprung from my only hate!' she gasped, for a moment appalled by it. But she would not let this evening's magic be dimmed! She gave no eyes to anything but the masked stranger, who departed with a backward look of longing that answered her own.

Benvolio and Mercutio had left the party and seen Romeo go on ahead of them. Now they could find him nowhere. They called. They teased. 'Romeo! Madman! Passion! Lover!' Mercutio called. He tried to conjure him by all the tricks that he could muster: by Rosaline's bright eyes, by her high forehead and her scarlet lip (for they knew nothing of the swift flight of Romeo's old love and the instant birth of his new). But still Romeo was nowhere to be found, and so, rollicking with good cheer and bawdy humour, the two friends rolled on their way home.

Yet Romeo was near, and heard them. He had gone ahead and on an impulse leapt the wall into old Capulet's orchard. Shocked by this surge of daring, he hid from his friends' mockery. Now, in the darkness, he crouched down, not knowing why he stayed or what he hoped to do, but propelled by that same unseen power of fascination towards the house where dazzling Juliet lived.

It was as if the darkness was suddenly aflame, for Juliet stepped out onto her balcony, and then it seemed to Romeo's eyes as though she was the sun rising to flood the world with glorious light.

An impulse pushed him forward, then he held back. He struggled with the wish to run to her and then to hide in shyness and just drink in the wondrous vision.

Juliet, on her balcony, was unaware of watching eyes. She sighed loudly, for she was wrestling with the misery of knowing that her passionate stranger was a Montague.

'Deny your father,' she begged, as though Romeo lodged somewhere in the rustling tree-tops. 'Refuse your name! Or if you will not, be my love and I'll no longer be a Capulet. It is your name that is my enemy. Oh, be some other name!' she addressed the moon and stars. 'What's in a name! If we call a rose by any other name it would smell as sweet. So would Romeo were he not called Romeo. Romeo, throw off your name, and take all myself!' she cried, abandoning herself to this secret dialogue with unseen love.

Romeo broke from the shadow of the wall. 'Call me but love,' he cried, 'and I'll be new baptized, I will be Romeo no more!'

With a cry Juliet fled back into the shadows, aghast at being watched when she believed she was alone. But realizing who the secret visitor was, she stepped forward, timidly, peeped, grew bolder and moved to look down across the balcony wall and see him.

'If my family sees you, they will murder you,' she warned him, softly, but letting her eyes caress his face so warmly that he felt armed against any Capulet dagger.

So they stood there, bathed in the moonlight that silver-tipped the fruit-tree tops, drunk with their new-made vows of love. For Juliet's heart was yet untapped, and though she knew her father brewed a marriage with Paris for her, she was bewitched by this mysterious young man who had, unasked, pierced the seclusion of her life, broken all the boundaries that divided this ancient, hate-locked city, and crossed forbidden territory to her side. *This* was not a love wrapped up in good sense and handed to her by a father, mother, Nurse, or any other. *This* love was hers, and even as they gave their first vows to each other, it entered her soul with a fierce passion that would never go.

'My bounty is as boundless as the sea,' she cried. 'My love as deep; the more I give to you, the more I have, for both are infinite!'

Romeo knew he could live in the magic of this night for ever. It seemed as though he had drifted from a wilderness in which he ached always alone, a pilgrim in a thankless search for love: (how long it seemed to be since he had thought he ached for Rosaline!). But now it was as though his whole existence led towards this single night, and nothing could exist outside. All time was now, he and Juliet locked in their bond of faith; there was no future and no past, except with her.

Quickly, before the world intrude with the dawn and take from them anything of their sworn love, he hurried to a monastery outside the city walls to see the monk, Friar Lawrence, who knew him well.

The friar was shocked to find young Romeo already up, and quickly guessed he had not been to bed that night. But learning that this excess of energy was not devoted to the lovely Rosaline, he was amazed to hear another girl had stolen in to take her place. He shook his head. Young men's love did not lie truly in their hearts, but in their eyes! What a tide of tears had Romeo shed for Rosaline, and look now – forgotten!

Romeo would have no scoldings at his fickleness. He had a single-minded purpose now. With all the speed that he could muster, Friar Lawrence must marry him to Juliet, and marry them today!

The friar stared, half disbelieving what he heard. This doting youth was so changeable he could not keep up with him! Yet, watching Romeo prowl up and down in a restless torment of excitement, he hoped that perhaps some deeper flame now spurred his young friend on.

Well, perhaps he should perform this marriage for the youth. Perhaps Capulets and Montagues would even cancel out their hate when such a love could fly the boundary between them!

Benvolio and Mercutio were puzzled. They had not seen Romeo since he left the feast, and he had not gone home that night. Yet they knew that Tybalt, the angry Capulet, had sent a letter to Romeo's house challenging him to a duel for insolence in coming to their ball!

'Romeo will answer it,' said Benvolio, certain of his cousin.

'Alas, poor Romeo!' mourned Mercutio, clasping his heart. 'He is already dead, stabbed with a young girl's black eye, shot through the ear with a love-song . . . And is he a man to encounter Tybalt?'

'Why, what is Tybalt?' Benvolio enquired.

'More than a prince of cats, I can tell you,' Mercutio waxed lyrical in scorn. 'He is the very butcher of a silk button, a duellist, a duellist, a gentleman of the very first house, a man of fancy thrusts and lunges,' and he mimicked the self-important prancing steps of Tybalt.

But here came Romeo to interrupt their joke. And what a change there was! No longer the mooning youth of yesterday, but the Romeo of old, so quick and apt to exchange the cut and thrust of jest with them that Mercutio retired defeated from the contest, pleased to see his friend so thoroughly repaired in spirits. And so they strolled on, chatting, while Romeo nursed his precious secret knowledge and looked for some messenger from Juliet, for she had said that she would send one.

And here came Nurse, puffing across the square, fanning away the steaming heat, and pressing on, for though she knew that Capulet had already promised Juliet to Paris, her old heart warmed to this tale of secret love and she thrilled to be Juliet's messenger to Romeo.

Entrusted in the care of Nurse, then, Romeo sent word to Juliet. She must find some way to come to Friar Lawrence's cell that very afternoon. There the holy friar would marry them at once.

Juliet paced up and down as though every minute was an hour and every hour a day until she heard from Romeo. A thousand terrors filled her heart: perhaps the Nurse had not found him; perhaps she brought bad news; perhaps he'd change his mind and did not love her . . .

But when she heard the news all terrors fled, and only the prospect of her union with Romeo lived in her brain. So many hours to go till then!

At Lawrence's cell, Romeo awaited her arrival with scarcely less intensity of hope: there was no sorrow could undo the joy he won from one short minute in Juliet's sight. 'Then love-devouring death do what he dare!' he defied the world. 'It is enough I may call her mine!'

'These violent delights have violent ends,' the friar chided him, 'and in their triumph, they die. Love moderately,' he warned.

But when Juliet came, with an airy step that floated on the cushion of her love, the friar's misgivings were instantly dispelled. Truly these young people loved!

'Come,' he hurried them, 'and we will make short work.' They must be married now, for such a pair should not be held apart.

The heat hung leaden in the streets, damp, cloying, maddening. Benvolio was nervous, for Mercutio was in a brazen mood, his wit stung to an irritable edge; and there were Capulets drifting through the streets looking for a fight. 'I pray you, good Mercutio, let's go in,' he begged. 'These hot days the mad blood is stirring.'

'Come, come, you are as hot in your mood as any in Italy,' Mercutio said restlessly, 'and as soon moved to be moody.'

'By my head, here come the Capulets,' Benvolio muttered.

'By my heel, I do not care,' retorted Mercutio, and turned his back on the approaching group.

'Gentlemen,' cried Tybalt, recognizing them as friends of Romeo, 'a word with one of you.'

'But one word with one of us?' said Mercutio, bristling. 'Couple it with something; make it a word and a blow!'

Belvolio tried to pull him back: away, into some private place to have their quarrel, for here all men's eyes were on them, and the prince had forbidden such brawling on pain of the heaviest punishment!

But Tybalt had lost interest in this sparring match, for he saw Romeo enter the square. 'Romeo!' he yelled. 'You are a villain!'

Romeo was fresh from his marriage to Juliet; he knew nothing of the challenge from this cousin of hers and he could find no anger in his heart even to rebuff the open venom of the words. 'I am no villain,' he spoke mildly. 'Therefore, farewell. I see you do not know me.'

'Boy,' spat Tybalt, ripe with insults, 'this shall not excuse the injuries you have done me. Therefore turn and draw your weapon!'

'I do protest,' persisted Romeo, 'I never injured you.' Even now his head was filled with nothing other than his marriage; it made him now a cousin to this Tybalt who pranced so desperately in search of a war. 'So, good Capulet, which name I hold as dearly as my own . . .'

Mercutio turned on his friend in disbelief. What had become of him, so calmly, so *dishonourably* to submit to this puppet duellist's taunts? Well, he would take the wretched insult up!

'Tybalt, you rat-catcher,' he yelled, and drew his sword.

And suddenly there they were, circling like wild cats . . .

'What would you have with me?' snarled Tybalt.

'Good king of cats, nothing but one of your nine lives . . .' jeered Mercutio.

'Gentle Mercutio, put your sword away,' urged Romeo.

'Come sir,' Mercutio egged Tybalt on.

'Tybalt, Mercutio, the prince expressly has forbidden fighting in Verona streets,' Romeo cried out. 'Hold Tybalt! Good Mercutio!' and he stepped towards his friend to beat his weapon down. Swiftly Tybalt's sword shot beneath his uplifted arm and into Mercutio's side.

Mercutio clutched the wound. 'What, are you hurt?' gasped Romeo.

'Aye, aye, a scratch, a scratch,' winced Mercutio, and turned suddenly very pale. 'Go fetch a surgeon,' he breathed, grey with pain.

'Courage, man,' urged Romeo, 'the hurt cannot be much.'

'No, it is not so deep as a well, nor so wide as a churchdoor, but it is enough, it will serve . . . Ask for me tomorrow and you shall find me a grave man.' Mercutio gasped, and staggered a little, reaching for Benvolio's arm. 'I am done for this world,' he cried. 'A plague on both your houses! A dog, a rat, a mouse, a cat to scratch a man to death!' he yelled at Tybalt. 'Why the devil did you come between us, Romeo? I was hurt under your arm.'

In stricken misery, Romeo stared at his friend. 'I thought all for the best,' he whispered. The black hatred that was so swiftly stealing Mercutio's life now seemed to gather about Romeo and push him on, and with a cry of fury for Mercutio he leapt on Tybalt, fighting with a demon passion before he could think again; and before the onslaught, murderous Tybalt fell dead.

Romeo looked at his bloody sword. He looked at Benvolio's white-faced panic, urging him to fly before the prince should come, for it was death for anyone who broke Verona's peace.

'Oh, I am fortune's fool,' gasped Romeo. Wed to Juliet only an hour ago, and now the killer of his wife's cousin! Love and Juliet should be beckoning him, now only death or flight could wave him on!

Even as he fled the square, the Prince of Verona came with soldiers, and with Montague and Capulet. Bitterly these enemies demanded

justice for their side. 'For blood of ours, shed blood of Montague,' raged Juliet's mother. 'I beg for justice, which you, prince, must give. Romeo killed Tybalt. Romeo must not live!'

The prince looked at her in silent anger. *Mercutio* was no Capulet or Montague felled by their hatred! He was the prince's kinsman. He should have been beyond the reach of this vile feud. Would this poison *never* end? From now on he would be deaf to all the pleas these Capulets and Montagues used so easily to excuse the bitter fruits of enmity! As Romeo had been stung to this brawl by Mercutio's death, so would he reduce the sentence of death: but to a punishment no less complete.

Romeo was banished from Verona for ever more, on pain of instant death should he return.

Juliet knew nothing of the fight. She knew only that she loved, and that night would bring her husband to her bed.

'Come, gentle night,' she coaxed, 'come, loving, black-browed night. Give me my Romeo; and, when he shall die, take him and cut him out in little stars and he will make the face of heaven so fine that all the world will be in love with night . . .'

She turned eagerly to Nurse, who seemed to bring some news. But there was something wrong! No joyous ecstasy at imminent wedding nights from Nurse, but wringing hands, and wailing words! "Tybalt dead and Romeo banished!"

Banished! Juliet struggled to understand the word. 'To speak that word is as if father, mother, Tybalt, Romeo, Juliet, were all dead. "Romeo is *banished!*"' she cried. The man she longed to see, to love, to hold, gone from Verona for ever more!

At Friar Lawrence's cell Romeo too heard the prince's sentence on him. And he knew that banishment meant death, for it was banishment from Juliet, from life itself!

The friar spoke calming words: banishment was only banishment from Verona! 'Be patient,' he urged. 'The world is broad and wide.'

'There is no world without Verona walls,' cried Romeo.

'This is dear mercy from the prince,' protested Lawrence.

'It is torture,' wildly Romeo rejected it. 'Heaven is here, where Juliet lives, and every cat and dog and little mouse may live here in heaven and look on her, but Romeo may not!'

In vain the friar tried to calm his black despair, but Romeo would hear none of it. What could the friar know? He was not young, in love with Juliet, married a short hour, killer of Tybalt, and now *banished*. What could the friar know of such depths of hopelessness?

But now the Nurse came hurrying in with messages from Juliet. She waited in desperate loneliness to see Romeo before he had to go. Nurse and Lawrence urged him to go to her; but he must leave for Mantua before the dawn. And then the friar would make his marriage to Juliet known, try to reconcile the families and obtain a pardon from the prince, so that Romeo could come back to bask in happiness!

His spirits much revived by this hopeful plan, and armed with the friar's promise that he would send word to Romeo in Mantua, of Juliet, in Verona, Romeo went to meet his love.

Capulet was worried by the grief that seemed to seize his daughter at Tybalt's death. Knowing nothing of the secret marriage to Romeo, he could not guess the true cause of her unhappiness, and he thought it sprang from far too deep a well of sorrow. He was anxious for his daughter's health, and wished to have her misery gone. What better way than to occupy her mind with being wed! What better way than to have her married, and quickly, too, to Paris! Having so made up his mind, he picked the day and told it to his astounded wife. On Thursday next, in two short days, Juliet would marry Paris.

'Go to Juliet, before you go to bed,' he told Lady Capulet. 'Prepare her, wife, for this wedding day.'

But Juliet was already locked in her wedding night with her new husband, longingly denying the birdsongs of the dawn that would take him away from her.

'I must be gone and live, or stay and die,' murmured Romeo, yet hoping she would entice him back for one last minute of happiness.

'That light is not daylight,' she whispered back. 'I know it, I. It is some meteor that the sun throws out to be your torchbearer and light you on your way to Mantua.'

'I have more care to stay than will to go! Come death, and welcome,' Romeo cried, and folded her inside his arms.

But already the sky was paling and with the anxious arrival of the Nurse, come to hurry them along, he pulled away and began to climb down from the balcony into the orchard. Was it just one short day ago that he had first exchanged his love with Juliet? He seemed now to have known her all his life!

He saw her pale face looking down and heard her paler whisper. 'Do you think that we shall ever meet again? Oh god, I think I see you, now you are below, as one dead in the bottom of a tomb! You look so pale.'

'And trust me, love, so do you. Dry sorrow drinks our blood.'

And then he was gone, nothing but the echoes of the night still in her ears and on her lips and in her arms.

A call startled her. Lady Capulet was at her door! Why was she up at this strange hour? So late not to be in bed: so early to be up already!

Lady Capulet had much to tell, despite the hour: she had a scheme to follow Romeo, the killer of Tybalt, to Mantua with poison. Soon, he too would die. And other tidings which she delivered with all the certainty of Juliet's pleasure: in two days time she would be wed to Paris!

Juliet heard it through a mask: she let no look, or word escape to tell of her love for Tybalt's killer, nor that she was a wife before ever Paris could lay claim on her. Half in terror at the trap she saw, half in terror at her parents' anger when they knew, she cried, 'I wonder at this haste! I pray you, tell my father that I will not marry yet.'

'Here comes your father; tell him so yourself and see how he will take it at your hands!' her mother told her angrily.

'What, still in tears?' her father demanded brusquely. He turned on his wife in irritation.

'Have you delivered to her our decree?'

'Aye, sir, but she will none. She gives you thanks. I wish the fool were married to her grave!'

'How!' bellowed Capulet. 'Is she not proud? Does she not count her blessings, unworthy that she is, that we have brought so worthy a gentleman to be her bridegroom?'

'Not proud you have,' protested Juliet, in tears, 'but thankful that you have . . .'

'How now, how now! What is this?' her father yelled. '"Proud" and "I thank you" and "I thank you not". Thank me no thankings nor proud me no prouds, but prepare yourself for Thursday next to go with Paris to St Peter's Church or I will drag you on a hurdle!'

'Good father, I beg you,' wept Juliet, 'hear me with patience.'

'Disobedient wretch! I tell you what: get to church on Thursday or never after look me in the face: speak not, reply not, do not answer me; my finger's itch! God's bread,' raged Capulet. 'It makes me mad: day, night, hour, tide, time, work, play, alone, in company, all my care has been to have her married: and having now provided a suitable gentleman, to have her answer, "I'll not wed, I cannot love, I am too young, I pray you, pardon me!" I do not jest,' he hissed at her, 'if you will not wed, you may hang, beg, starve, die in the streets, for by my soul I'll never take you in!'

Juliet sat trembling in the silence behind his departing back.

'Oh, sweet mother, cast me not away,' she begged. 'Delay this marriage for a month, a week; or if you do not, make my bridal bed in that dim monument of death where Tybalt lies!'

'Talk not to me,' her mother waved her off, 'for I'll not speak a word. Do as you will, for I have done with you.'

Juliet sank beneath a tide of hopelessness. All helping hands withdrawn! All roads to Romeo cut off and only one path open – marriage to another man!

She fled to Friar Lawrence's cell. The friar trembled at the dangers now looming before them all. A desperate plan took shape within his brain, fraught with a kind of horror. But Juliet was ready for anything to keep her faith as Romeo's wife. Friar Lawrence gave her a potion: drink it, and she would seem to die, while all the while she only slept. This sleep with the look of death would last for forty-two hours; so, when they came to rouse her for the wedding, they would think her dead! According to long-established custom, they would lay her body in the tomb where the bodies of all the Capulets lay.

Meantime, the friar would send word to Romeo in Mantua. Romeo would hurry to the tomb to greet her when she woke, and carry her away with him to safety!

Awash with sudden hope, Juliet seized the friar's potion and hurried to her room.

The household was in a flurry such as there had never been before. One more day to prepare a wedding feast! Old Capulet gave orders for the festivities, while watching for some change of heart in Juliet.

And so there seemed to be! She came from Friar Lawrence all smiles, begging his pardon, and saying she would now be ruled by him!

'Send for Paris,' Capulet roared in triumph. 'I'll have this knot knit up tomorrow morning.'

'No, not till Thursday,' Lady Capulet begged her headstrong husband. 'We will be short in our supplies: it's nearly night!'

But he would have no contradiction. 'We'll go to church tomorrow.' His heart soared, so light it felt now that his wayward daughter had seen the error of her ways.

Juliet was alone. The silence filled her with a faint cold fear, like the creeping chill of tombs to which she would shortly give herself. It almost froze the heat of life in her. So suddenly to be faced with this! No time to think!

A thousand fears grimaced in her brain: what if the friar's potion did not work? She seized her dagger and held it up: why then, this would have to do the task! What if she woke before she was rescued, trapped in a tomb with only dead people to keep her company? Perhaps the loathsome foulness of the air would strangle her, or send her mad . . .

She pushed the visions back, and with a rush of courage raised the potion. 'Romeo, I come,' she whispered to the silence. 'This I drink to you.'

In Mantua, Romeo knew nothing of all this. He neither knew of Friar Lawrence's secret potion to make Juliet *seem* dead, nor that her father insisted that she marry Paris now.

His servant brought him only the news that Juliet was dead, found lifeless on the morning of her marriage.

The words broke upon him like the ice of his own death.

'Is it really so?' he breathed. 'Then I defy you, stars! I will go there tonight . . .'

'Sir, have patience,' his servant begged. 'Your looks are pale and wild.'

Romeo brushed his worries off, and urged him away to find horses for the journey to Verona.

'Well, Juliet, I will lie with you tonight,' he told her, in his head. A plan had taken hold of him, and now he had no other purpose in his life. Quickly he found a man in Mantua to sell him a deadly poison. 'Come, poison,' he spoke softly to the fatal bottle in his hand. 'Go with me to Juliet's grave, for there I must use you.'

Friar Lawrence hurried to the tomb where Juliet lay, armed with an iron bar to open it. His heart pounded with misery and fright. The messenger he had sent to tell Romeo that Juliet was not dead, only asleep, had not reached him! Both messenger and letter had been put in quarantine against the plague, and only just released.

So now the friar hastened to reach Juliet. She would wake soon, alone, trapped in the tomb. He must rescue her before she died of fright! Then, he would write again to Romeo and keep Juliet in his cell until Romeo could come to take her.

'Poor living corpse,' he wept, 'closed in a dead man's tomb!'

There was another visitor to the tomb that night. Paris knew nothing of Juliet's love for Romeo, nor of her terror at the marriage planned with him. He wept to lose her on their wedding day, and he came to lay flowers on the tomb and weep his private tears.

A third figure was entering the graveyard shadows. It was Romeo, fired by a grim light within which made his servant tremble.

'Whatever you hear or see, stand well away and do not interrupt me in my course,' Romeo gave orders to his servant. 'Do not return and pry, or by heaven I will tear you joint by joint and strew this hungry churchyard with your limbs!'

'I will be gone, sir, and not trouble you,' the servant hastily assured him. But he hid, to wait, for fear of what his desperate master planned.

Paris, sheltering behind the Capulet tomb, saw only that the Montague who had killed Juliet's cousin and made her take her life, now tried to open the tomb and desecrate it. With a shout of rage, he drew his sword and rushed to stop him.

And Romeo, knowing only that no one must stop him reaching Juliet's side, brought the intruder down.

'Oh, I am killed,' Paris gasped. 'If you be merciful, open the tomb and lay me with Juliet.'

Romeo saw now who he had killed, and understood that this man too loved Juliet. Sorrowfully, he lifted him and carried him into the tomb, and laid him gently on the floor.

Then he rose, and climbed onto the cold stone slab where Juliet lay, and knelt with her. She lay so warmly beautiful. He did not see the crimson blush of her lips or fresh bloom of her cheeks as life, only as her beauty flaming for him even in her death. He could almost believe that Death itself loved her, and kept her in her glory here, to be his bride.

But Romeo would defy even Death, for he would stay with her and never leave this palace of dim night!

He lifted her then to his last embrace, sealed her lips with a kiss that would never end; and then he raised the poison to his lips and drank, and fell across her body, dead.

Friar Lawrence panted through the graveyard. He found Romeo's servant, and such a terror filled him as he had never known. He saw the bloodstains at the entrance to the tomb, the gory sword flung down, ran in and saw Romeo's lifeless corpse, and bloody Paris too.

Above this grim monument to death, Juliet began to stir. She saw the friendly face of Friar Lawrence, and smiled. 'Oh, comfortable friar, where is my lord? I do remember well where I should be, and there I am! But where is Romeo?'

Bereft of words, the friar shrank from the sight that greeted her waking eyes. He heard a noise outside, 'Lady, come from that nest of death,' he begged. 'Come, come away! Your husband lies there dead, and Paris too. Come, I'll put you in a sisterhood of holy nuns. Stay not to question,' he pleaded again. 'Good Juliet, I dare no longer stay.'

'Go,' said Juliet, 'for I will not away.'

A vast blackness filled her, as though the dark chill of death had already taken her. There was no world outside this place: no world beyond this tomb, where Romeo lay . . .

She found the cup of poison in his hand: no drop in it to help her on her way! She kissed his lips: no poison clung to them, only the warmth of life just gone.

But here his dagger waited, like a friend.

'Oh happy dagger!' she cried. 'This is your sheath!' and as the sounds of people running to the tomb broke in upon her world of timelessness, she stabbed herself and fell dead on Romeo, locked in her last embrace.

Capulet and Montague gathered around those they had buried with their hate. The sight of their children's deaths was like a bell that tolled their own deaths in this world of viciousness in which they revelled. And the sight of death was now the bell that tolled them back from it.

'Where be these enemies?' the Prince of Verona cried. 'Capulet! Montague! See what a scourge is laid upon your hate!' He looked at the body of Paris, so swiftly following Mercutio. 'And I too,' he mourned,

'for winking on your quarrels, have lost a brace of kinsmen. All are punished.'

But the tolling bell was heard by those who had till now heard nothing. Capulet reached a hand across to Montague. Each swore to raise a statue in pure gold in honour of the other's child; so would all know the tale of Romeo and Juliet, who fell before the venom of an ancient war, and only whose deaths had sounded the final call to peace.

King Lear

There was a king in Britain, once, named Lear, who had a long and fruitful reign; and so, as frail old age drew close to him, he longed to give up a monarch's cares and rest. But still he wanted to be king, for all his years upon the throne had taught him to enjoy the fruits of power. He was not ready, yet, to throw them off.

Among the abundant riches of his life he counted, above all else, his daughters. Three there were: Goneril, the eldest, married to the Duke of Albany; Regan, the second, married to the Duke of Cornwall; and the third, the one he loved the most, Cordelia, youngest and still unmarried, although the King of France and the Duke of Burgundy were even now at King Lear's Court as suitors for her hand in marriage.

And so, in seeking to throw off the heavy duties of his reign, King Lear prepared to give his kingdom to his daughters. The core of his design was known, but little more than that: precisely how he planned to carve up the country was not yet clear.

Even more strange than this, the king, it seemed, had planned a little contest: the size of each daughter's portion of the land would be decided by the amount of love that they declared for him before the Court!

Courtiers crowded in to see the spectacle. They knew how much the old king loved the pomp and show of ceremony. How would each daughter fare? What would they say? Yet the hearts of some who stood there, waiting, beat with something more than curiosity: a looming sense of doom weighed heavily upon the Earl of Kent, Lear's oldest friend. The old king seemed to think that this division of his realm would smooth away the cause of conflict between rivals for the crown after his death! Instead the loyal Kent saw what Lear refused to see . . .

The king swept in, close followed by his daughters, Goneril and Regan, and their husbands.

'Give me the map there,' commanded Lear, and held it up. 'Know,' he said in measured tones, and paused to give full weight to all his words. 'Know that I have divided my kingdom in three, and it is my intention to shake all cares and business from my old age . . .'

Cordelia lingered behind her sisters and the king. She did not like these games her father played. She loved him far too well, and loathed to see him toy with her, with others, with their lives and fates . . .

'Tell me, my daughters,' King Lear went on, 'which of you shall I say does love me most?' and he smiled benevolently on all of them: *he* knew how well they would acquit themselves before the Court, expressing their love in fulsome words so he could bestow their prizes on them now, for all the world to see how fully they deserved them for their loyalty to him.

'Goneril, our eldest born, speak first,' he commanded her. Goneril stepped forward. 'Sir,' she declared in ringing tones. 'I love you more than words can say; dearer than eyesight, space and liberty; beyond what can be valued, rich or rare; no less than life or grace, health, beauty, honour; as much as a child ever loved a father . . .'

Lear nodded. It pleased him well, and with his jewelled hand he swept across the map: rich forests, meadows, rivers, hills, all fell in a single stroke to Goneril, her husband and her children yet to come.

'What says our second daughter, our dearest Regan?' he demanded. 'Speak.'

Regan hurried to him, flushed pink in anticipation of her prize.

'Sir, I am made of the self-same substance that my sister is. In my true heart I find she names my love; only she falls short,' she threw her sister a look of triumph. 'I declare myself an enemy to all other joys, and can be happy only in your dear highness' love.'

Lear nodded again. She had done well. 'To you and to your children for ever more, I give this ample third of our fair kingdom.'

It was Cordelia's turn. 'Now, our joy,' he said, with pride, and turned her well-loved face towards him, triumphant in his expectation.

Silence followed. Dumbly Cordelia stared at him, her love for him erupting in an overwhelming misery. What should she do: love, and be silent? What was *he* doing? What did he *think* that he was doing? Taking these sisters' grand pledges of all-consuming love for real jewels! Giving this unsightly command to perform a ceremonial dance before a public court. And on *this* to settle the fate of daughters, kingdom, the people of the land! He should know *she* loved him, without this.

Lear looked at her impatiently. 'Speak,' he commanded. 'What can you say to draw a part more opulent than your sisters?'

Still Cordelia stared back at him. Her love was richer than her tongue; her father drew from her all the loyalty and warmth that her young nature had. But she *would not* play this game to which he stooped. She trembled at what she knew she was about to do.

'Nothing, my lord,' she said.

Lear's impatient pacing stopped. He swung round to look at her. 'Nothing!'

'Nothing,' Cordelia answered again, with thundering heart.

'Nothing will come of nothing,' warned her father, his tone becoming hot. 'Speak again!'

She looked through misting eyes at him, appalled. Why does this father that I love want this from me? Why does he think that love must be parcelled like a cake and given, all, to one person alone? I have love enough in me for him, for husband, children, all . . .

'Unhappy that I am, I cannot heave my heart into my mouth,' she said to him. 'I love you according to my bond; no more, no less.'

Her father thrust his face close up to her. 'How, how, Cordelia! Mend your speech a little, or it will spoil your fortunes!'

She tried to still the trembling in her voice. She *would not* be cowed because her father chose not to see what was before his very eyes.

'My lord,' she said, courage giving her soft voice an edge of steel, 'you have fathered me, bred me, loved me: I return those duties back as are right fit. I obey you, love you, and most honour you. Why have my sisters husbands, if they say all their love is yours? When I shall wed, that lord whose hand takes me shall carry half my love with him, half my care and duty. Sure, I shall never marry like my sisters to love only my father and no one else!'

But in the moment that she uttered this and saw the blank pain cloud her father's eyes, a kind of terror overwhelmed her. Sure, she had spoken the truth, but this father of hers would not see the vast love for him that gave her words their warmth and honour. He saw only the starkness of rejection. He did not see her love, he saw only disloyalty. He did not see her honesty, he saw only ingratitude and cruelty.

'So young, and so untender?' he questioned brusquely.

She flinched before the brewing storm. 'So young my lord, and true,' she said. There was a hideous pause, a total silence filled for Cordelia only by the rhythm of her thudding heart.

'Then let your *truth*,' the word exploded in her face, 'let your *truth* be your bridal dowry. Here I disclaim all my paternal care! As a stranger to my heart and me hold yourself forever! Begone from my sight!'

And with an enraged sweep of his hand Lear encompassed the whole boundary of Britain. Let his two other daughters take the third that should have been Cordelia's! Their loving loyalty was worth it all! In one great stroke before the horrified Court he gave Goneril and Regan the total power to act as rulers of his kingdom, his wealth, his palaces, his all. He kept only the name of king and one hundred knights to be paid for by his daughters from the wealth he gave them. And with each of these two, in turn, he would make his home till his life's end.

'Royal Lear,' the Earl of Kent pushed forward desperately to his side.

'Peace, Kent!' Lear warned him. 'Come not between the dragon and his wrath. I loved her most . . .'

'But what will you do, old man,' the Earl of Kent persisted, unflinching in the face of Lear's volcanic rage. 'Do you think that honest people should be afraid to speak when power bows to flattery? Reverse your doom. Check this hideous rashness. Your youngest daughter does not love you least!'

'Out of my sight!' Lear thundered.

'See better, Lear,' shouted Kent. 'I tell you, you are doing evil!'

Lear reached in blinding fury for his sword; there was a sudden move to stop him. But there was no going back: the Earl of Kent was blasted from Lear's heart. If on the tenth day from that time he were still found within Lear's kingdom, that moment would be his death!

So were the suitors for Cordelia's hand flung the discarded daughter of an outraged king. Who would have her now, demanded Lear contemptuously. What was she worth, without his love or wealth?

The Duke of Burgundy admitted that he sought her only for her promised wealth, and he withdrew. The King of France was made of different stuff. He saw only the honesty and strength of young Cordelia against the blinded folly of a vain old man. 'Is it not most strange,' he asked King Lear, 'that she, who until now was your best object, deserving all your praise, the best, the dearest, should in this trice of time commit a thing so monstrous as to dismantle all your favour?'

'Better you had not been born than not to have pleased me better,' muttered Lear to Cordelia, with a look as dark and vicious as his words.

'Fairest Cordelia,' the King of France reached for her hand, 'you are most rich, being poor. You will be queen of our fair France. Bid them farewell. You lose here, only to find a better place . . .'

'*You* have her, France, for *I* have no such daughter, nor shall I ever see that face of hers again.' Lear turned his back and swept away.

Cordelia stood before her sisters. 'The jewels of your father,' she said quietly. 'I know what you are: and like a sister I am most loathe to call your faults as they are named. Treat our father well.'

'Do not tell us our duties,' Regan dismissed her coldly. And Cordelia went. The two sisters were alone, each triumphant in her new-found wealth. Each now controlled a half of this great land, half its power. They eyed each other, measuring the other's will and strength.

'I think our father will leave here tonight,' said Goneril. And, testing how her sister would respond, 'you see how full of changes his age is. He always loved our sister most, and with what poor judgement he has now cast her off.'

'It is the weakness of his old age,' Regan agreed in scornful tones. 'But he has always little understood himself.' Above all, they knew he was a man given to great shows of strength and power, bred in him by the ease of being king so long. How long before such rashness as they had seen this day against Cordelia would find its target in them . . .

'We shall think further on it,' Regan murmured, her voice swelling with unsaid meaning.

Goneril nodded. 'We must do something, and soon.'

This was not the only strife that brewed between a father and his child that day. The Earl of Gloucester had two sons. One was Edgar, born of Gloucester's wife, nurtured as the son who would inherit all his wealth and lands and be the Earl of Gloucester after his father's death.

The other son was Edmund. He was *not* born of Gloucester's wife nor conceived in the marriage bed, but on a casual night of lust many years ago with a woman whom Gloucester had barely known and now had almost forgotten. For years he had pretended that this Edmund was no son of his. But now the young man came and planted himself before his father's eyes and would not go away. Gloucester, being older and less given to shrugging off his duties than when he was a younger man, resigned himself to admitting that Edmund was, indeed, his son, but with such sly nods, with bawdy jokes about young Edmund's mother, making clear that while this Edmund was a son, he was only a *bastard* son; Edgar was the *true* heir to all of Gloucester's wealth.

Edmund listened to it all, his face a handsome mask on which no watching eye could read the pattern of his thoughts. But beneath that smooth, unruffled mask there was a bitter scorn that rankled deep. Such contempt and anger he felt for Gloucester! 'Bastard' his father called him! Since he was a tiny child, as far back as his childhood memories could stretch, he knew he had loved Gloucester and longed to be loved by him and called a son. Yet the only name that Gloucester used was 'bastard!' Why bastard? Why? In this world, it seemed, a man was measured not by his merits, skills or wits, but by his *birth*: birth of a noblewoman was noble, rich and prized; birth of a common woman was common, base, rejected . . .

And then there was his brother Edgar: so comfortable in all his father's love, so certain in his birth and in the rights and wealth that came from it! Well then, brother, Edmund thought, I must have your lands. Edmund, 'the base' would top Edgar, the 'true' son! Edmund

52

'the base' would grow, would prosper, would seize all!

And so Edmund carefully brewed his plan. He caught his father even as the old man reeled with the events at Court that day. Gloucester shuddered. Surely the cloud of some dreadful impending doom glowered in the skies above. He could feel the chill already seeping through his bones. And here came Edmund with a letter! (He seemed to try to hide it, but Gloucester finally managed to persuade him to give it up.) And what was this? Young Edgar's handwriting! Gloucester began to read, scarcely believing his eyes. 'Tired of his father's aged tyranny' the letter said! They could divide the dead Earl's money between them!

It was a plot to kill Gloucester and to seize Edgar's inheritance before its time!

Edmund, he saw, tried to spare him the pain of Edgar's treachery, but here, in his own hand, he held the proof. His own beloved Edgar, his own true son, plotting against his life! Gloucester stumbled away from Edmund, his mind a hornet's nest of panic, bewilderment and anger. Could a well-loved, trusted son be such a monster?

Edmund smiled. This letter, which he had written, all, himself, had planted fears in fertile soil! Now to sow a matching fear in brother Edgar's heart and so speed his plot along the road to fortune.

He found Edgar reading quietly, as he often did. Had Edgar displeased their father in some way, Edmund enquired with concern. How angry Gloucester was! He was talking of banishment and death! Edgar would be wise to keep away until he, Edmund, could quieten the old man down; he feared for this brother's life.

Such talk and rumblings of violence and punishment! Edgar could not think! Confused, becoming instantly afraid, he fled to hide, as Edmund advised him to.

Edmund smiled again in satisfaction. How fast his arrows shot towards their target! A father who knew so little about his sons that he was ready to believe this most extraordinary tale, and a brother whose unsuspecting gentle nature was so far from doing harm that he could smell no trap even when it reeked beneath his nostrils.

So, if Edmund the bastard son could have no lands by birth, he would at least gain them by wit!

Goneril seethed with resentment against her father. Idle old man, who wanted still to manage those things that he had given away! He seemed to think her home was all his own! Day and night he argued with her. Day and night he quarrelled with her servants, even striking one of them for telling off his Fool, this Court Jester who seemed to have been given licence by the king to spew out what insulting cheek he pleased!

And worse, this noisy train of knights who jaunted through Lear's useless days of pleasure with him. A hundred knights! A hundred men to feed and clothe! Their riotous noise infected her whole Court. Everything the old man did, surrounded by this unruly band of men, seemed to Goneril to clip her fledgling wings of power.

She gave commands. Let all her servants treat the king's loud knights with colder looks; let them *not* be ready to serve them, when they called. She would write to sister Regan, at once, advising her to do the same when Lear and his retinue came to her next month. So would the old man learn that he lived now only by *their* courtesy!

'Dinner, ho, dinner!' roared Lear, returning ravenous from hunting. 'Where's my Fool? Go you,' he told a passing servant, 'Call my Fool!'

He thumped the table, loud. 'Where's my daughter? Where's my

Fool? I think the world's asleep!'

But here came the fool now, slowly, with pale face and downcast eyes, not like the merry boy he usually was!

'I marvel what kind of people you and your daughters are,' he murmured mournfully. 'They'll have me whipped for speaking true, you'll have me whipped for lying; and sometimes I am whipped for holding my peace. I had rather be any kind of thing than a Fool: and yet I would not be you, nuncle,' he told Lear. 'You have pared your wit on both sides and left nothing in the middle.' He turned as Goneril strode into the room. 'Here comes one of the parings . . .'

'Not only, sir,' Lear's daughter's voice shook with anger, 'not only this your all-licensed Fool, but others of your *insolent* retinue do hourly shout and quarrel . . .'

'Are you my daughter?' Lear interrupted her. How *dare* she speak to him like this!

'Come, sir,' said Goneril impatiently, 'I wish you would make use of that good wisdom that I know you have and put away this misbehaviour that transforms you . . .'

Lear stood in disbelief at what he heard. He'd never listened to such arrogance before! The daughter of a king speaking to a king and father as though he were a misbehaving child! He began to shout. 'Does anyone here know me?' Swinging round he yelled it at his knights who lounged about the hall. 'This is not Lear: does Lear walk like this, or speak like this?' he demanded, slouching like a lazy servant. 'Who is it that can tell me who I am?'

'Lear's shadow,' murmured the Fool, drawing close behind his master and staring defiantly at Goneril's icy face.

Her eyes flashed now with unconcealed contempt. 'Understand me,' she hissed at Lear. 'You are old. You should be wise!'

Lear barely heard her now. There was a sudden drumming in his brain, like the rhythm of a hammer beating, blow on blow. Reduce the number of his knights, she said! Behave!

'Darkness and devils,' he roared. 'Saddle my horses! Call my knights together! I'll not trouble you,' he shouted back at Goneril. 'I have another daughter left!'

Ingratitude! Was this the daughter he had thought so deserving of her father's lavish gifts? 'Oh Lear, Lear, Lear,' he struck his head. 'Beat at this gate that let your folly in and your dear judgement out.' How could he think that Goneril loved him? Let her live long enough to feel how sharper than a serpent's tooth it was to have a thankless child!

Yet he had another daughter left: Regan! 'When she hears of this,' he hurled at Goneril, 'with her nails she'll tear your wolfish face!'

Goneril no longer listened to the explosion of her father's rage. She pondered instead the number of his knights. A hundred! It was not sensible to let one old man keep armed a hundred knights, for with their powers he could shore up the idiocies of old age, follow each complaint, dislike, each dream or fancy . . . Regan must also refuse to harbour this quantity. And, if she should decide to *sustain* Lear and his knights, why, then Goneril would know she brewed some other purpose!

She brushed aside her husband's protests. Albany was far too mild! If he could not see the danger to themselves in Lear surrounded by a hundred loyal knights, all armed . . . well she would see it for him.

Lear trembled before the storm that rumbled in his brain. That Goneril should use him like this! To Regan now, quick, for she would set the world to rights again! And here again was that stout servant who had come that very day to Lear and insisted on staying near, to serve him. Send *him* with messages to Regan, and with all possible speed!

'I will not sleep, my lord, till I have delivered your letter,' the servant said, and took it, but with a heart as heavy as the king's. For though King Lear had not recognized the face behind the stubbled chin and work-worn clothes, nor known the voice masked by a heavy country tone, this 'servant' was none other than the banished Earl of Kent, come back, disguised, to stay beside his king as he had always done. Someone must try to save old Lear from being crushed beneath the ruins of his world! He had thrown away his power and his Cordelia, and now he tried to build a universe upon the love of daughters such as Goneril and Regan! How swiftly, within two weeks, had Goneril bared her serpent's tooth. Holding the power she had long sought, now she stripped away all pretence at love or duty and left only the raw antagonism of one who aimed for absolute power and would have no interference with it.

Lear paced beside his Fool, waiting restlessly for horses to be ready. Again and again the same refrain beat through his head. He had given *everything* to Goneril, and what was she giving in return? The thought was like a wound across his brain, wracking him with hurt and anger.

The Fool saw where Lear's thoughts were going and understood.

Since Lear had sent Cordelia away, the Fool had felt the sunshine leave the court, and now there were only dark skies hovering above them all. What a king this was! How blind could one, all-powerful person be? The Fool's heart flooded with sorrow for them all, and for this old, old man who in such stupid vanity had released the horror. Swiftly he skipped and danced about his king to try and patch his temper up.

He thrust his small, thin face close to the wrinkled one and demanded with a perky look, 'can you tell how an oyster makes his shell?'

'No,' said Lear, who was not listening to the Fool but to the rumblings of swelling thunder that seemed to be within his head.

'Nor I neither, but I can tell why a snail has a house,' said the Fool.

'Why?'

'Why, to put his head in it; not to give it away to his daughters and leave his horns without a home,' came the saucy answer.

But Lear did not hear it. So kind a father he had been! What monster ingratitude in Goneril! And suddenly he thought of Cordelia in France, and the thought brought with it an unutterable pain. 'I did her wrong,' he moaned. Quickly the Fool put his arm about the old king's shoulders, and felt them shrunken beneath his ample robes.

'If you were my Fool, nuncle,' he said gently, 'I would have you beaten for being old before your time.'

'How's that?' asked Lear distractedly.

The Fool leaned his head against the grizzled beard of Lear, and wished that he could weep. 'You should not have been old till you were wise,' he said.

Lear's head ached. He could not think. Regan: all would be well once he was with his Regan.

'Oh, let me not be mad,' he whispered. 'Not mad, sweet heaven! Keep me in temper; I would not be mad!'

Edmund's grand design progressed. So swiftly had he planted panic in his brother Edgar's heart, that already Edgar had fled from Gloucester's wrath, while Gloucester stormed about the castle in a frenzy of offended rage. A beloved son, to plot the murder of his father: this monster would be sought in every corner of the land!

Edmund, for his loyalty in bringing the treachery of Edgar to his father's eyes, would be well rewarded . . .

That night, with little warning and great haste, Regan and her husband the Duke of Cornwall came to Gloucester's castle. Letters from Goneril had warned them of her quarrels with King Lear. Letters from Lear had reached them, too. But Regan was of the self-same mind as Goneril. Why should a dispossessed old king be allowed to wield the power of armed knights? It was not sensible.

Edmund watched this daughter of the king and her husband, Cornwall, carefully. Already, within two weeks of Lear's division of the kingdom, he had heard talk of wars brewing between this Duke and Goneril's husband, the Duke of Albany.

But for the moment it was *this* Duke, and *this* daughter of Lear, who stood here in his father's castle. With these two Edmund would join, for so his climb to power would be the faster.

Meanwhile the loyal Kent had gone with all the speed that he could muster to Regan's palace. Finding Regan and her husband gone to Gloucester, he followed them. Now, before the Earl's great castle, he saw another messenger who made his skin prick with fierce anger: the messenger from Goneril!

'Draw, you rascal! You come with letters against the king!' he cried.

With a yelp of terror, Goneril's messenger leapt back. Out rushed Edmund with drawn sword, followed by the Duke of Cornwall and Regan. The king's messenger brawling outside the gates! Here was a sample of the king's unruly followers just as Goneril had written!

'Fetch the stocks,' the Duke of Cornwall ordered. 'We'll teach you.'

'Call not your stocks for me,' warned Kent. 'I serve the king!'

There was a gleam of glee but thinly masked in Regan's eyes. To punish the king's messenger publicly: it was a timely opportunity! He should stay there the whole night through, pinioned in the stocks.

'Put in his legs,' she ordered.

And so the rebellious Kent was fastened in the wooden stocks and left. But the loyal Earl had something rich to warm the hours of waiting for the king. He pulled it from his pocket and held it up to catch the sunlight. A letter, from one who held as firm a course of love for Lear as he did: Cordelia. She had been told of Kent's nearness to the king, and Kent knew that from this daughter there would be help.

Edgar, in flight, was terrified. On all sides he heard his father's servants call his name. Nowhere was safe for him to go, for Gloucester had ordered the death of anyone caught aiding his fleeing son.

One refuge there might be: to hide among the multitudes of half-mad beggars who roamed the countryside, their twisted limbs shored up with bits of wood, bared to the winds and howling in their desperation for some paltry gift of food. Among these he could melt away, for nobles such as Gloucester were always blind to wretchedness like this.

And so it was that Edgar, son of the Earl of Gloucester, became a beggar, his face begrimed with filth and knotted hair, shunning all company and known to those who saw him peering from his hovel as 'Poor Tom', whose wits were gone.

King Lear was struggling to understand. Regan and her husband Cornwall departed from their home! No message left for him and his own messenger not sent back! It was most strange.

He followed them to Gloucester's castle. But what a sight was there to greet him! *His* messenger, imprisoned in the stocks! Some vile mistake had been made.

'Who has so misused you as to put you here?' he challenged Kent.

'It is both he and she,' Kent said, wearily. 'Your daughter and her husband.'

'No,' said Lear.

'Yes,' said Kent.

'No, no,' Lear whispered, trying to shake the truth away. 'They would not. They dare not do it. They could not, would not do it.'

'I tell you they have,' said Kent.

'Where is this daughter,' Lear cried suddenly, and beat at the gates of Gloucester's castle until the Earl appeared.

His daughter denied to speak to him! They were sick! They were weary! 'Fetch me a better answer,' he told Gloucester.

'My dear lord,' Gloucester tried to calm him, 'you know the fiery quality of the Duke of Cornwall . . .'

'Fiery!' bellowed Lear. 'What quality? Why, Gloucester, Gloucester, I would speak with the Duke of Cornwall and his wife. The *king* would speak with Cornwall. The dear *father* would with his *daughter* speak. Are they informed of this?'

His eye fell on Kent still in the stocks, and somewhere within there was a quivering knowledge pushing upward through his mind.

'Give me my servant,' he roared, finding release in rage, for now his heart beat like the thunder that would overwhelm him and beat him to oblivion. But here was Regan! It was all over, at last. He hurried to his daughter, putting out his hand.

'Beloved Regan,' words tumbled out of him. 'Your sister's tied sharp-toothed unkindness, like a vulture, here,' he thumped his heart. 'I can scarce speak to you . . . you'll not believe it, Regan.'

With a sharp lift of her hand, Regan shook him off.

'I cannot think my sister in the least would fail her obligation,' she said. 'You are old. You should be ruled and led by some discretion. I pray you, go back to my sister and say that you have wronged her, sir.'

Lear halted, uncomprehending horror flooding over him. 'Ask her forgiveness?' he whispered, and could not move. Then the slow burn of fury began to fill the wound in him and suddenly he dropped to his knees and wild sarcasm fired his mocking words. 'Dear daughter, I confess that I am old; on my knees I beg that you will give me clothing, bed and food.'

'These are unsightly tricks,' Regan said. 'Return to my sister.'

'Never, Regan,' shouted Lear. 'She has torn away half my train of knights, looked black upon me; struck me with her tongue upon the very heart. Let all the stored vengeance of heaven fall on her ungrateful head! Strike her bones with lameness . . . !'

Through his rage he saw that Goneril had come, and Regan was hurrying to her side. She took her sister's hand and stood beside her, looking haughtily towards her father.

'Oh heavens,' whispered Lear raising his eyes to the sky, 'if you do love old men, send down and take my part.'

'Father, as you are weak, seem so,' he heard Regan's voice.

There was a sudden gust of wind that seemed to shake the castle walls, a wail that almost drowned the tempest rising in Lear's mind.

He barely heard the sisters now. From one to the other the vile negotiation flew: dismiss half his followers, then he could go to Goneril. After, when Regan was *ready* to receive him, he could go there.

Lear held his hand before his eyes so that he did not have to look at Goneril. 'Daughter, do not make me mad. I will not trouble you, my child.' He turned his back. 'Farewell. We'll no more meet, no more see one another . . .' All, all he had given them, and now they bargained his followers against himself. Fifty, at a stroke, to go, said Goneril; now twenty-five more, said Regan; now not one to stay.

'I gave you all, made you my guardians,' he whispered. 'You see me here, a poor old man, as full of grief as age, wretched in both!'

He swung in sudden fury to look at them again. 'I will take such revenges on you both . . .' he strode up and down, 'I will do such things . . . *you* think I'll weep! No, I'll not weep.' He saw the Fool's ashen face watching him in terror. 'Oh, Fool,' he whispered, 'I shall go mad.' There was the scream of bitter winds beyond the walls, and trees whipped low, and it was like the tempest roaring in his head. Away, away, at all costs away from them . . . He fled, the Fool running after him and Gloucester following with a glance of pure dismay.

Regan looked at Goneril, 'I'll receive him gladly,' she said, measuring her words with care. 'But not *one* follower.'

Goneril nodded assent. A weak old man, alone, they could give room to. A king with loyal followers, they could not.

Gloucester was rushing back wringing his hands in desperation at his powerlessness. The night was coming on and such bleak winds were blowing. For many miles there was no bush to give an old man shelter, and the king was out in this!

'Shut up your doors,' said Regan.

Gloucester looked from her to Cornwall in disbelief.

'Shut up your doors,' said Cornwall. 'It is a wild night.' He looked hard at Gloucester, defying him to disobey his orders. 'My Regan councils well. Come out of the storm,' he said, and each word was measured like a hammer blow.

It was as though the world was coming to an end, as though a thousand years of rage was pouring from the heavens on a devastated earth. In the tempest two figures could be seen, the one staggering to and fro in fury to outshout the storm, the other struggling in sodden misery by his side, trying to outjest the wildness of the old man's rage and draw him back inside, out of the storm.

'Blow, winds and crack your cheeks!' Lear cried into the gale.

'Oh nuncle, good nuncle, let's go in,' pleaded the frozen Fool. 'Here's a night that pities neither wise man nor fool!'

'Rumble your bellyful!' yelled Lear to the skies. 'Spit, fire! Spout, rain!' flinging his arm out wide and letting the water pour in wild, gusting torrents down his face. Let the rain and wind and thunder bellow! They were not his daughters! He never gave them kingdoms nor called them children! They owed him nothing! 'Here I stand,' he cried, 'a poor, infirm, weak and despised old man. I ; .n a man more sinned against then sinning,' he shrieked.

Now came old Kent battling through the storm to find them, urging them towards some shelter: *anything* to shield them from these icy sheets of rain or surely the old king would die before the night was through. Nearby was a hovel . . .

Lear stopped. He trembled, and whispered to himself, 'My wits begin to turn.' Then he saw the drenched misery of the Fool and flung his arm about the boy's frail shoulders.

'My boy, are you cold? I am cold myself. Come,' he said to Kent, 'take us to your hovel. Poor Fool,' he murmured again, with almost forgotten softness in his voice.

And with Kent leading through the black fury of the night, Lear with his arms about the Fool, the Fool sang loudly to keep their spirits up:

'He that has and a little tiny wit,
With a hey, ho, the wind and the rain.
Must make content with his fortunes fit
For the rain it raineth every day.'

Inside the castle walls Gloucester spoke in secret to his son. 'I have received a letter this night. It is dangerous to speak of it.' And in low voice he told of an army from Cordelia and France that gathered on the coast of Britain to help the king. 'We must help him,' he declared, 'though I may die for it!'

With barely concealed impatience, Edmund watched him hurry out. A plan, so daring that it almost horrified him, had formed even as he listened to his father. This information from Gloucester would be given *instantly* to Cornwall. Would not Cornwall, learning from Edmund that Gloucester helped the king, would not Cornwall in a single stroke of fury chop down the Earl of Gloucester and raise up his son?

Lear stood in awe before the hovel. It crouched so wretchedly beneath the forked fires tearing through the skies. He stared in disbelief at ragged roof and gaping holes all open to the winds. Did *people* live in this? Did poor wretches have to suffer the pelting of this pitiless storm in *this*? As though a window opened in his mind, he saw all his years as King of Britain rushing like a torrent past his eyes. 'I have taken too little care of this,' he groaned, for storm without and storm within were reaching a shattering crescendo in his head as years of knowledge blindly pushed aside erupted in a searing rush of vision.

A curdling shriek tore through the gale. 'Help me, help me!' howled the Fool and rushed into Lear's arms. A naked man was leaping after him, glistening grotesquely in the rain, screaming as though all the devils in hell were after him!

Lear's brain could hold no more. It sank beneath the savagery of this unnatural night. 'Have you given all to your daughters?' he shouted to the naked man. 'And have you come to this? Could you save nothing? Did you give them all?'

'He has no daughters, sir,' Kent said gently, trying to take Lear's arm.

Lear stumbled towards the gibbering wretch who still twitched and yelled and fought a thousand invisible horrors off his back.

'Nothing could have brought him to such lowness but his unkind daughters,' insisted Lear.

'This cold night will turn us all to fools and madmen,' muttered the Fool with chattering teeth.

'Take heed of the foul fiend,' the shivering madman cried. 'Tom is cold,' and he plunged into the shadows.

'Is man no more than this?' Lear gasped. Such a poor, bare, forked animal. 'Off, off,' he yelled and began to tear away his clothes.

'Nuncle,' the Fool protested faintly, 'be contented. It is a naughty night to swim in.'

There came another leaping yell and the madman ran from the red flare of a torch that swayed towards them through the hissing night. For the madman saw who carried it: the Earl of Gloucester, come to find the king. And the madman hid his face, for he was no madman but Edgar, the outcast son of Gloucester, hiding as 'Poor Tom'. Frantically he scrabbled back into the hovel and away from Gloucester's prying eyes.

'Go with me,' Gloucester pleaded with the king. 'I cannot obey your daughter's hard commands. I can bring you to where both fire and food are ready.' Lear paid little attention. 'Poor Tom' had seized his churning mind. He would go nowhere without 'Poor Tom'.

'His wits begin to unsettle,' murmured Kent with dread.

'Can you blame him?' whispered Gloucester. 'His daughters seek his death. I tell you, friend, I am almost mad myself. I had a son, now outlawed from my blood. He sought my life. I loved him, no father loved his son dearer. Truth to tell, the grief has crazed *my* wits.'

'Tom is cold,' mumbled the naked man, still keeping his face turned from his father's unseeing eyes.

Inside the shelter of the castle walls, Cornwall nursed a purpose darker than any Gloucester could have guessed. The Duke knew now of Gloucester's deeds, and of the army coming to aid the king. For his loyalty in telling Cornwall this, young Edmund was now Earl of Gloucester in his father's place . . . and Cornwall waited, festering for his revenge upon the insolent old Earl who had so dared to disobey.

Inside the shelter of a farmhouse near the castle, warm and dry, a trial was taking place: the judges were the Fool, 'Poor Tom' and Kent. Lear was giving evidence.

'Bring in Goneril,' he commanded grandly, and placed two stools before the judges. 'I here take my oath before this honourable assembly, she kicked the poor king her father.'

'Come here, mistress, is your name Goneril?' yelled the Fool, his spirits high with warmth and ready now to humour the king's mad game.

'She cannot deny it!' rejoiced Lear. He pointed to the stool. His daughter shook with guilt!

'I'm so sorry,' the Fool bowed elaborately, 'I took you for a stool!'

Edgar, hiding behind the false madness of 'Poor Tom', almost wept to see this real madness in the king.

'Good my lord,' Kent tried to quieten Lear. 'Lie here and rest . . .'

The lull was brief. Gloucester returned. He had overheard a plot of death upon the king! Kent must take him instantly to Dover where the powers of Cordelia and France would protect them. Loyal knights would meet them on the road. Not even half-an-hour's delay, or Lear's life, their lives, the lives of all who helped him would be lost . . .

In the castle another trial began. 'Bind fast his shrivelled arms,' Cornwall gave orders as Gloucester reached his door.

'Good my friends,' protested Gloucester. 'You are my guests and in my house; do me no foul play.'

'Bind him, I say!' was all the answer Cornwall gave.

'Hard, hard,' cried Regan and plucked his beard viciously. 'So white and such a traitor,' she taunted him.

In that instant Gloucester understood: there could be no escape from these vultures' vengeance. Like claws their words ripped into him.

'Where have you sent the lunatic king?'

'To Dover,' he declared defiantly.

'Why to Dover, sir?'

A sudden anger fired his courage, 'Because I would not see your cruel nails pluck out his poor old eyes, nor your sister stick her boarish fangs into his royal flesh. But I shall see the winged vengeance overtake such children,' he yelled.

'See it, you never will,' hissed Cornwall. With a hand like a ravenous beak he plunged his fingers into Gloucester's eye and tore it out.

The shriek of agony tore through the castle walls and a bloody cavern stared at the grinning torturers.

'The other, too,' urged Regan hungrily.

'Hold your hand,' a servant cried, hardly believing what he'd seen.

'How now, you dog!' spat Regan and stabbed him through the back.

'My lord,' the wounded man cried out, 'you have one eye left to see some mischief done on him!' and with his dying breath he plunged his sword into the Duke of Cornwall.

Nothing would stop Cornwall from his bloody purpose. Clutching his gushing wound he lurched towards Gloucester. 'Out, vile jelly,' he yelled, and clawed his fingers round the other eye and held it up . . .

Gloucester moaned. Edmund, where was Edmund?

Regan's laugh rang shrill. 'You call on him that hates you,' she rejoiced. '*Edmund* told us of your treason!'

Gloucester heard, but did not understand. His unseeing face turned towards the woman, then towards the man. And then the pain of understanding shot through him like a knife-thrust. In the agony of darkness behind the bleeding cavities that should have been his eyes, Gloucester saw what he had never seen before. His Edgar was innocent. Edgar was loyal.

'Go thrust him out and let him *smell* his way to Dover,' Regan said.

Far from the sight of their vile mistress and her bloody Duke, the gentle hands of servants took the tormented man and soothed his wounds with whites of egg. They bound the gaping holes and led him quickly from that place of savagery.

They took him to 'Poor Tom', for no one would stop a madman leading a blind old man away. So it was that Gloucester fell into the hands of Edgar, his outlawed son. And Edgar, who in this world of Goneril and Regan should have burned for revenge on a father blind to truth, wept to see the broken man, whose only purpose left was to climb the highest cliff and end his blighted life by plunging to his death.

'I have no way, and therefore I want no eyes,' moaned Gloucester. 'I stumbled when I saw.'

Cornwall was dead, killed by that swordthrust from the servant who would rather die himself than see the torture of another man.

Like monsters of the deep who live only to devour each other, the sisters turned more murderously on each other than on anyone else: Goneril glowed with a new greed, for Edmund, the handsome Earl of Gloucester. Regan lusted for him too, and with her husband dead, she would let nothing stand between her and her union with this man!

Edmund swore his love to both of them. Either, or both would raise him up. Either, or both, might help him mount even to the throne of Britain! He played with both of them, like toys. Let the strongest win!

The Duke of Albany was far from the savagery of Gloucester's castle. He could barely believe the story his servants told of that night's grotesque events. How could he not have seen this monstrous *thing* that was his wife, till now? What viciousness had been unleashed since that strange day when Lear had ripped his kingdom up and handed it to daughters such as these! Tigers, not daughters!

Cordelia had reached Dover. So little time had passed since she had left this land, and yet how far this monstrous waste of evil spread. She had known her sisters. And yet she had not known them: in her wildest thoughts she could not have imagined this.

She longed to see her father, to bind up the wounds that turned his mind to stumbling insanity. But Lear would not consent to see Cordelia. He was consumed by such remorse and shame for what he'd done to her that he fled wildly from her soldiers as they looked for him.

In the fields near Dover two wandering figures could be seen. The one staggered across the muddy ground with tattered bandages binding the gore that had once been his eyes. The other moved close by his side, held out a hand to help him, lifted him whenever he fell, and spoke quiet, encouraging words to keep him moving on his way. 'Poor Tom' had brought the Earl to the high hill he asked for, or so Poor Tom told Gloucester. Look how steeply the ground climbed up! Could he not hear the sea? Seabirds wheeled on the cliff-side far below and there the fisherman on the beach was little bigger than a tiny mouse! Why, Gloucester was standing on the very edge and if he leapt he would surely dash his brains to pieces!

So was the blind man persuaded it was really so, and giving everything he had to this poor beggar who had so faithfully led him here, he knelt and asked forgiveness of the gods, asked a blessing for his lost son Edgar, and threw himself forward through the air, but fell only a few feet onto the muddy ground of Dover's field and lay there, no longer knowing if he lived or died.

Edgar ached to see the pitiful desperation in his father. Swiftly he helped him up, persuaded his confused and trembling mind that he had truly leapt from a great cliff-top but that the gods had spared him. A miracle! And with his calming words Edgar began to smooth away the hopelessness that gripped his father.

But what was this? A tottering, skipping thing, bedecked in flowers and crowned with weeds! It capered across the fields towards them. Though his eyes told Edgar it was the king, his brain could not admit it.

'Ha! Goneril with a white beard,' Lear did a little dance towards them. 'They flattered me like a dog,' he assured them both, yet recognizing neither. 'They told me I was everything! It is a lie!'

'The trick of that voice I do well remember,' gasped Gloucester. 'Is it not the king?'

'Aye, every inch a king,' King Lear assured him, and he flung his arms out wide, revolving with a stately pace before his little audience. 'A man may see how the world goes with no eyes,' he nodded to Gloucester. For in this twisted world where daughters plotted murders on their fathers and evil people could pass judgement on the innocent, where wisdom and goodness were vile things to be stamped on, torn out or blinded, so there was also another truth that maddened Lear had sniffed his way into: that in all this chaos of injustice there were also honest women and honest men and where their honesty was found, so it would survive and grow to challenge every hour the monstrous waste of those who let their greed loose to devour all others in their path.

Now Lear saw that soldiers came across the field to find him, and he capered off again with saucy backward glances, not understanding that these soldiers came from Cordelia, sent in love to bring him back to her.

Edgar was alone again with Gloucester. Still Gloucester did not know that this beggar who stayed so firmly by his side was the lost son he mourned for.

'Give me your hand,' said Edgar to his father.

And Gloucester gave it.

Cordelia watched her sleeping father. If only a single kiss from her could sponge away the havoc of her sisters' poison. She saw the old man stir, and backed away in shyness. The doctor urged her forward again.

'How does my royal lord? How fares your majesty?' she murmured.

Lear struggled from sleep such as he had not had for many days. Sleep had stilled the storms and calmed the fury in his head that would have dashed him to pieces on the rocks of his insanity.

He saw Cordelia. A scarcely-believed new hope began to stir. 'Pray, do not mock me,' he murmured, and wiped his hands across his blurred eyes. 'I am a very foolish, fond old man, and I fear I am not in my perfect mind. I think I should know you, yet I am doubtful.' He saw the clothes he wore, and this room in which he rested, but he did not know them, for gentle hands had bathed his battered body, clothed him in clean garments and led him to rest . . .

In some confusion he looked into her face. 'Do not laugh at me,' he whispered. 'For I think this lady is my child, Cordelia.'

'And so I am, I am,' Cordelia almost wept to watch the confusion and understanding warring in the old man's face.

'If you have poison for me, I will drink it,' he said, 'I know you do not love me: your sisters have, as I do remember, done me wrong. You have some cause, they have not.'

'No cause, no cause,' said Cordelia, and clasped her arms about his neck. And then she gently raised him up and led him to walk quietly by her side. Lear leaned heavily on her arm, a great calmness falling over him, for now his head began to understand, his heart to move, his limbs to strengthen. Cordelia! His Cordelia! She had come to him. Her love had not been poisoned by the wrongs he had done her. A great light and peace shone from her, and folded him inside its warmth. He had given nothing to her and taken everything away, but *still* she gave her love. Such was the miracle that his many years upon the earth had never made him see before. This love was not a parcel to be bought and sold; it was a richness greater than all his royal possessions had ever been.

Edgar was fighting for his father's life. Edgar, who had fled in terror from all weapons, was forced now to pit his life against a murderer sent by Regan to kill Gloucester. But Edgar brought the attacker down. With his last gasp the stranger asked him to take a letter from his pocket and, without fail, deliver it to Edmund. So it was that Goneril's messages to Edmund came into Edgar's hands. He read, but could hardly believe: Goneril begged Edmund to kill her husband Albany! Free from him, she could outpace Regan in Edmund's love.

Now these serpents came to war against Cordelia: Regan and her army, led by Edmund, matched with the army of Goneril and Albany. Edmund watched the Duke of Albany with irritation, for he had not yet declared himself against Cordelia. Would he, or would he not fight her?

Albany's honest conscience struggled with the madness of his choice. He could not let an invader's foot advance onto Britain's soil. He would be forced to defend a kingdom against an invading army, knowing that invader held up the cause of honesty and love against the savagery of Goneril and Regan! But for the moment, Albany made his choice: to fight the foreign army which came behind Cordelia. Yet his final loyalty was to King Lear and Cordelia.

Goneril and Regan rode together, each festering with a rabid jealousy that obscured all else. Goneril watched Edmund ride as commander of her sister's force, and knew that she would rather lose the battle than that her sister should steal Edmund's love.

Edmund weighed the possibilities before him. To both women he had sworn his love. Neither could be enjoyed if both remained alive. And as for this conscience-stricken Albany, well, his support was needed in the battle. But once the course of war was run . . .

The savagery of war followed the savagery of greed and raged across a smoking land; it left only the twisted ruins of people's lives, the broken bodies, gaping eyes and torn carcases strewn in its monstrous wake.

Cordelia's army, fighting for Lear, lost. Goneril and Regan, their forces led by Albany and Edmund, won. Edmund knew that Albany would treat the vanquished king and daughter with some mercy and moved fast against them, giving orders that they should be taken from the field as prisoners before Albany came.

'Come, let's away to prison,' murmured Lear to Cordelia. 'We two alone will sing like birds in the cage: when you do ask my blessing, I'll kneel down and ask of your forgiveness. So we'll live, and pray, and sing, and tell old tales . . . Wipe your eyes,' he told her. 'We'll see them starve before they'll make us weep.'

So they went: Cordelia who should have been in France, wrapped safely in the warmth of a new husband's love, not standing in the bloody field of battle bound in ropes; and Lear, whose battered mind held only the ecstasy of being with Cordelia.

But Edmund sent swift, secret orders after them: without delay, they should both be killed.

Albany came to find them. Finally he had learned the full depths of evil to which his wife and Edmund stooped: before the battle, a stranger had thrust a letter in his hand. He had not recognized Edgar in disguise, but had agreed to grant his odd request: to read the letter, and if he won the battle, to let the herald sound a trumpet for a champion who could prove the truth of what it told.

So Albany had learned of Goneril's plot against his life, and now he came with thunder in his heart.

'Edmund, I arrest you on capital treason, and with you this gilded serpent!' he cried, and swung contemptuously to face Goneril.

A hot gleam shone in Goneril's watching eyes as Regan turned white with sudden pain, and swayed, clutching her stomach.

'Let the trumpet sound,' challenged Albany.

'My sickness grows upon me,' Regan moaned again.

'She is not well, convey her to my tent,' commanded Albany, his eyes never leaving Edmund's face.

Edmund was drunk with power. What man could challenge him! He rode too high on this day's crest of victory.

Once, twice, three times the trumpet rang.

There came an answering call. Before their astonished gaze a stranger stepped out, his face and body clad in armour, a trumpet in his hand.

'You are a traitor, false to your gods, your brother and your father; conspiring against this high-illustrious prince. This sword, this arm, are bent to prove it!' he cried.

Edmund defied any man to topple him from the heights he had reached. He leapt to the challenge with all the certainty of victory. But

71

the stranger fought with the passion of a thousand men, and beneath his driving onslaught, Edmund fell.

Goneril ran towards her fallen lover. 'Most monstrous!' Albany held up her letter. 'Do you know this paper?'

Goneril halted. She looked from the letter in her white-faced husband's hand to the fallen Edmund, bleeding on the ground. She backed away, her face working with thwarted hate, turned, and fled.

Edmund struggled up to see the stranger who could so turn the wheel of fortune against his rising star. The stranger threw off his helmet.

'My name is Edgar, and your father's son!'

Edmund sank back. Brother against brother it was now, just as the story had begun. Through a mist he heard his brother's tale: how he had led their blinded father, never revealed who he was until a half-hour past: as he came towards this final conflict he had told Gloucester. His father's heart, too weak to take the shock, had burst between the warring flames of joy and grief, and he had died, smiling.

Edmund heard, and a shimmering note was rising in his head, a call to forgotten love, to once-remembered loyalty.

But like a trumpet's bray that heralded his own, the news of his lovers' deaths burst in upon him: Goneril had stabbed herself and fallen on the body of Regan whom she had already poisoned.

'I was contracted to them both. All three now marry in an instant,' Edmund whispered. A churning sense of urgency was taking hold of him. He struggled to sit up and saw, through blurring eyes, the Earl of Kent appear, come in search of Lear.

At the sight of Kent, Albany remembered. 'Speak Edmund, where's the king, and where's Cordelia?' he urged.

The calling cry in Edmund's head pierced through his dying brain now, harsh and clear. *Yet Edmund was beloved*, it seemed to say. *The one poisoned the other for my sake and after killed herself.* There was a rushing pulse in him, a last surge of honesty not yet drowned by his restless hunt for power. 'I pant for life,' he cried. 'Some good I mean to do in spite of my own nature! Quickly send to the castle, for my orders are against the life of Lear and Cordelia!' And Edmund died.

But King Lear had come to them. In his arms he held Cordelia. The fresh bloom of her young face was greyed, her arms and legs hung limp.

'She's gone for ever,' came Lear's howl. 'I know when one is dead and when one lives, and she is dead as earth.'

He lowered her body to the ground and knelt to press his face against her lips. Just *one* more breath, *one* more sigh of life to give him hope. 'Lend me a looking glass,' he begged. 'If her breath mists or stains the stone, why then she lives!' He gasped, 'The feather stirs! She lives!'

Then he saw her, dead, and all hope plunged. 'A plague upon you, murderers, traitors all! I might have saved her, now she's gone for ever. Cordelia, Cordelia! Stay a little,' his life swelled to this single need.

'I killed the traitor that was hanging you,' he told her with sudden pride. But she would come no more. Never, never, never, never, never, he hammered at the knowledge.

He saw then, finally, what he had done to her. His heart burst with the anguish of lost hope, and in one great rush of understanding at the waste of this, her stolen life, Lear fell across his daughter's body, dead.

The old Earl of Kent stood in silent, weeping homage above his king. His task was done, and he could hear the call of his own death. heralded by the fleeing life of his old, tired, royal master.

Albany and Edgar stood together. To them now fell the rule of this gored and stricken land. Greed and the lust for power had known no bounds and swept all else before it. Was there a lesson here for young to learn from old, and old from young? And who was going to learn it?

Albany raised his head and looked at those who had survived the holocaust in Lear's great land. 'We that are young shall never see so much, nor live so long.'

Othello

The two men moved between the arches, soft-footed in the shadows along the walls. Iago walked in front, talking in quick, sharp tones; close behind him scuffled Roderigo, straining to hear his every word.

They had a single purpose, and their goal was near at hand. They moved steadily across the dark expanses of the square between the sleeping houses; Iago slid into the shadow of an arch and motioned Roderigo on, into the light of torches at the entrance to Brabantio's house. Roderigo began to protest, then thought better of it and obeyed Iago's nod.

He turned his face up to the window. 'What, ho, Brabantio! Signior Brabantio! Ho!' he yelled.

Shrouded in the shadows, Iago raised his cry. 'Awake! Brabantio! Thieves! Look to your house, your daughter and your bags! Thieves!'

Brabantio's face, grotesquely startled from his sleep, thrust from the window high above their heads.

'Signior!' yelled Roderigo, warming to the task. 'Is all your family within?'

The old man peered into the ill-lit square. Who were these two? The one he recognized, that idiot Roderigo who haunted his door, mooning for his daughter, Desdemona. The other man he could not see . . .

'Are your doors locked?' Iago cried. 'Sir, you've been robbed. Your heart is burst, you have lost your soul! Even now, right now, an old black ram is tupping your white ewe! Your daughter and the Moor . . .'

Fear pierced the sleep-sodden face of the old man. 'Give me a light!' he roared. 'Call my people! Light, I say, light!'

And as the cry was raised in panic through his house, amid the flare of torches and the sounds of running feet, Iago melted off into the shadows. He could rely on Roderigo now to fill out their scheme a little,

74

to play upon this father's terrors for his fair white daughter, stolen off into the lover's arms of black Othello, the Moor.

Iago had other, urgent tasks, which could not be pursued if he were seen here, where the seeds were being sown against the Moor. He must fly back to stand beside Othello, to show the flag and sing of love, for was he not the trusted ensign of this noble Moor? Was he not *honest* Iago, outspoken, true and indispensable at his great master's side?

This Moor, so abhorred as a mate for his fair daughter by the Senator Brabantio, was a man of some considerable repute in Venice: of royal Moorish blood, a soldier, famed for military success, known for his nobility, his wisdom, experience and skills. There was no other general could lead the Venetian forces in the wars in Cyprus against the Turks.

So why then did Iago plant and nurse these seeds of venom against the Moor? Did even Iago know? He had always hated Othello. Contempt for this most powerful black man was woven round Iago like a skin: he moved always within it. One grudge could no longer be distinguished from another; he could not say which fed the next, or which was the spring from which the others flowed. True, Othello had not made him his lieutenant, his second in command – a post for which he was well qualified by skill, experience and long-standing service beside the Moor. Othello had instead preferred another, one Michael Cassio, and Iago remained his ensign, the lowest rank of officer.

Yet this grievance only served to fire already smouldering flames. He hated this most honoured Moor, gigantic in his reputation and his power. He hated: and he sought some satisfaction in his hatred. But no small punishment would be enough: it must be grand, colossal, monstrous in its finality . . .

Yet such a fertile climate blew its balmy air about the Moor. He was adorned in glory, decked with riches by the Venetian state for services in war. Each senator felt keenly how the health of their state depended on Othello's skills and reputation in these dangerous times of war.

And today he had secretly married the daughter of the senator, Signior Brabantio, the same senator that Iago and Roderigo had so rudely wakened from his sleep.

But Iago was ripe to poison the Moor's delight, and to begin with this night's work. With swift foot and still swifter tongue he reached Othello to tell of Brabantio's rage and imminent attack on him.

Othello listened with only half an ear. He could not easily be moved by such a tale. Everything he saw and heard this night was coloured by his love for Desdemona. And he knew, with the much-practised eye of a seasoned soldier and campaigner, that his vast services to Venice spoke far louder than any rage against him for this marriage.

He waited calmly for her father. But others reached him first: his lieutenant, Michael Cassio, with officers of the Duke of Venice, requesting his immediate attendance at a full session of the Senate on matters concerning the wars in Cyprus.

But suddenly there was a rumbling murmur in the streets about them and the ominous flare of torches carried by many men: Brabantio and his friends approached with weapons drawn, led on by Roderigo.

'Down with him, thief!' Brabantio was shouting.

Cassio and his companions instantly drew swords to defend Othello.

Othello did not stir. He raised a hand above the uproar.

'Keep up your bright swords, for the dew will rust them,' he said, and his deep, unhurried tones dropped across the tumult like a rich cloak to douse rebellious flames.

'Foul thief! Where have you stowed my daughter?' Brabantio shouted, incensed by this further proof of Othello's devilish powers. Already the Moor had used them on his daughter, for what other cause than this black witchcraft could make her shun the suitors of her own kind and fly to the black bosom of such a man as this?

'Damned as you are,' he shouted, 'you have enchanted her! You have practised on her with foul charms, abused her delicate youth with drugs or minerals. Lay hold upon him! If he resists, subdue him at his peril!'

The Moor stood quietly. No thought could be traced upon his face. He made no move as swords were raised against him, except that single motion of the hand which compelled the weapons down again.

'Where do you want me to go to answer this your charge?' he enquired softly of Brabantio.

'To prison,' the old senator spat his reply.

But now the Duke's officers intervened impatiently. The Duke's summons was being ignored. They were all wanted at the Senate, now: Othello and the senator, Signior Brabantio.

Brabantio was suddenly satisfied. The Senate, in full council session in the dead of night could hear his cause!

'The Duke himself, or any of my brothers of the state cannot but feel this wrong as if it were their own,' he said. Where would this end? If such a man as this could seize a Venetian daughter, why, pagans and bond-slaves would become Venetian masters!

Iago followed his general out. His face spoke volumes of anxious worry at this woeful ending to Othello's day of happiness. He was appalled at this attack upon the honour of his master.

But his inner thoughts were of a very different colour . . .

The Senate was in uproar. Letters had arrived, each widely different in the scale of their report, but all agreeing that a Turkish fleet was moving to attack the Venetian colony at Cyprus and instant reinforcement of the island's garrison was needed. Only the General Othello could be sent for such a weighty task.

But Brabantio's grief intruded even on questions of such vital importance to the state. He forced his fellow senators to hear: his daughter had been abused, stolen from him, corrupted . . .!

By whom? In consternation the senators saw his finger pointed at the Moor on whom their hope of fortune in the wars now rested!

The Moor nodded. He *had* married Brabantio's daughter. He addressed the accusations of the father with the courtesy due to a man of Brabantio's age and rank, but with a glow illuminating his face that all could see. 'Send for the lady,' he said. 'Let her speak of me before her father.' And while the senators waited for her to come, he spoke to them of how the gentle daughter of Brabantio had learned to love him; and as he told them, his face was captured by the wonder of the memories: he relived each look, each word, each blush . . .

'Her father often invited me,' he said, with a slow look at fuming Brabantio. 'He would ask me the story of my life from year to year, the battles, sieges, fortunes that I have passed. I spoke of most disastrous chances, of moving accidents by flood and field, of being taken and sold into slavery, of vast caves and idle deserts, rough quarries, rocks and hills, whose heads touch heaven . . .'

And so the Moor spoke on, the rich tapestry of his enormous life moving across his face and enriching every line and bone of it. Closer and closer still the tale had drawn Brabantio's daughter, Desdemona; she had given him a world of sighs for the pains that he had suffered.

'She loved me for the dangers I had passed, and I loved her that she did pity them. This,' he turned now to the senators, 'this is the only witchcraft I have used.'

'I think this tale would win my daughter too,' the Duke of Venice murmured, with a smile.

And Desdemona, entering with her exquisite face aglow as was the Moor's, had eyes only for Othello. Though she addressed her father in loving tones, her words told only of her final, absolute loyalty to this, her chosen husband, lord and love, the Moor.

Iago knew then his scheme had foundered on the rocks of Desdemona's love and Othello's faith in her. His hatred burned a little higher. There was no simple trap to catch this man. It needed a web of infinite proportions, woven with the utmost skill . . .

'Look to her, Moor,' he heard the thwarted father mutter. 'Look to her, if you have eyes to see; she has deceived her father, and may deceive you.'

'My life upon her faith,' Othello dismissed the father's words, and turned to flood his wife with all the richness of his loving gaze.

In the silence of the Senate court after they had gone, Roderigo sulked. He had hoped Iago's scheme to separate Desdemona from the Moor would open the field to him again. 'I will drown myself,' he muttered piteously.

'Come, be a man! Drown yourself? Drown cats and blind puppies!'
Iago put his arm about Roderigo's shoulders, comfortingly. Though
this first stab had not pierced its target as he had hoped, he would still
have his need for an ally such as Roderigo. 'Put money in your purse,'
he urged him. 'Follow these wars. Desdemona must get bored with the
Moor! She must yearn for some change from him . . .' and if Roderigo
were near at hand, in Cyprus, well . . . !

New hope flickered across Roderigo's disappointed face. 'No more of
drowning, do you hear?' Iago prompted him.

'I am changed,' enthusiastically Roderigo assured his friend, rushing
off. 'I'll go sell all my land!'

Alone, Iago could feel the threads of a design that gathered in his
mind. He searched about for them: a web to spin that would ensnare
them both, Othello and the favoured Cassio. He searched, and searched
again, and heard that tolling bell . . . Desdemona! At the centre of his
design, this gem would be the bait.

The threads still floated, unconnected in his mind, their ends
free . . . and then in a moment they had caught, and knitted, and he
had it: the idea! He would make Othello think his gorgeous, faithful
wife was locked in some faithlessness with Cassio . . .

Othello commended his new wife to Iago's care, and before the break of
dawn, set sail with Cassio for Cyprus. Iago, accompanying his own wife
Emilia and Desdemona, prepared to follow in another ship.

But raging storms that lashed a foaming sea to mountains and dashed
great ships to splinters, brought strange results: it wrecked the Turkish
fleet and finished all threat of their attack. The Venetian ships, though
driven wide apart, survived, and finally reached Cyprus.

And so they gathered on the island, like flies to Iago's spinning web.
Cassio's ship came first. Then came Iago with Emilia and Desdemona.
And finally Othello, hailed by a jubilant population as the hero who
would deliver them from all menace of the Turks.

But Othello had no eyes for any but his Desdemona. There could not
be a wonder greater than this overwhelming joy to see her again, no
calm so absolute as he felt, gazing on her now and she on him, longing
to rest in each other's arms and close the world away.

Iago watched. How well-tuned they were for him to play on! And so too was Roderigo, who had sailed for Cyprus and who lingered, like a love-lorn puppy waiting for a kick, to catch a glimpse of Desdemona.

First, he must tune up Roderigo. With swift strokes it was accomplished. Did Roderigo see this Michael Cassio? Not only had he usurped Iago's place as second in command, but he had also usurped Desdemona's love! She loved *Cassio* now, bored as she was with the coarse qualities of the Moor! So, (he explained the position point by point as Roderigo's brain could hold so little at a time) now Cassio had her; until *he* was removed, there was no hope for Roderigo.

'Be ruled by me,' he encouraged him. 'Watch tonight. Cassio does not know you. I'll not be far from you. Find some occasion to anger Cassio. He is rash and very sudden in his anger, and may strike you.'

And so the first thread was spun: jealous Roderigo was to deal with Michael Cassio. Now, on to the Moor. He must put the Moor into a jealousy so strong that judgement could not cure it. And he would use Cassio, with a single stroke to bring down a double enemy.

There was much feasting and jollity that night in Cyprus. A double celebration: the destruction of the Turkish fleet, and great Othello's wedding. For having set sail from Venice on the same night that he had married, his first union with Desdemona would be here on Cyprus.

He left the garrison in Cassio's capable hands, and Cassio would command the island's guard with Ensign Iago's help.

And what a jovial fellow this Iago was, Cassio soon found out: quick with a jest, a song, full of good humour and generous with wine to drink Othello's health, (though Cassio resisted strongly, for he had no head for drinking). Others came to join them: merry souls, among them Signior Montano, the governor of Cyprus who had sent for Othello's help. He too brought wine . . .

It was not very long before good Michael Cassio's speech grew slurred. He staggered a little, though he protested loudly that he was not drunk. He could quite clearly see his left hand, here his right, and here his ensign, good Iago! He stumbled away, earnestly assuring them that he could do his duty as well as any sober man . . .

As Cassio left, Iago's face became a mask of sorrow. What a vice this drunkenness was in a man, he murmured to Montano. Cassio was so fine a soldier, so trusted by Othello, yet every night he was like this . . .

Iago had seen Roderigo skulking in the shadows and was busy

signalling in secret to him to follow Cassio. Just as he had planned it, drunken Cassio now blundered through their midst in hot pursuit of Roderigo, throwing wild blows and kicks at him, and furiously waving his sword.

Montano instantly leapt up to catch and calm him; so enflamed with drink was Cassio that he merely yelled and staggered, swinging his sword wildly at the governor, and pierced him through the arm.

All the while Iago drew Roderigo off, seeming to give chase. 'Away!' he hissed. 'Go out and cry mutiny!' Within minutes the hideous clamour of a bell rang out the warning of a mutiny and panic spread like fire through the town.

'*Hold*, for your lives!' Othello's tones boomed like a cannon across the uproar.

Stung from his wedding bed by the noisy clamour, Othello surveyed them all in sheer disbelief. What barbarous brawl was this? What dreadful bell clanging to turn the island's people to blind terror! He rounded on his ensign. 'Honest Iago, speak. Who began this?'

Iago would say nothing, though his face was creased with grief.

Cassio, swaying in drunken stupor, could say nothing.

Montano? He was a man reputed for his seriousness! 'Worthy Othello,' he gasped. 'I am hurt. Your officer, Iago, can inform you.'

Othello, at first no more than startled, now grew angry. His officers and his guard brawling, with weapons drawn! 'Give me to know,' he said, with low and menacing voice, 'how this foul rout began. What! In a town of war, yet wild, the people's hearts brimful of fear, to follow private and domestic quarrels in the night! It is monstrous! Iago, who began it?'

'If you deliver more or less than the truth you are no soldier,' Montano panted to Iago, and nearly fainted with his wound.

A pain seemed to shadow Iago's face.

'I had rather have this tongue cut from my mouth than it should do offence to Michael Cassio,' he said. And haltingly, as if each word were a new hurt upon a loyal friend, he let out the tale: Cassio had pursued some stranger, Montano had stepped in to calm him, he himself had chased the fleeing stranger (who had quite outrun him). 'Yet surely,' he added, 'Cassio must have received from him that fled some strange insult which patience could not support.'

Othello looked long and hard at Iago. How clearly he could see that Iago's honesty and love tried to put less blame on Cassio!

Cassio steeled his spinning brain to receive the general's wrath. But there was no wrath. Only the quiet, damning words: 'Cassio, I love you well. But never more be an officer of mine.' Othello turned and left.

Cassio sank to his knees. The full meaning of what had just been said now pierced the haze that clouded his sodden brain. He almost wept.

'Reputation, reputation, reputation! I have lost my reputation! Iago!'

Iago rushed to him with swift concern. 'As I am an honest man, I thought you had received some wound! There is more sense in that than reputation!' he dismissed the sacked lieutenant's blank despair.

But all was not lost, Iago was convinced of it. Cassio, he said, must simply approach the general, make amends, and get his position back. And why not try to win the help of Desdemona, for there could be no voice more powerful to move the Moor . . . 'Beg her help to put you in your place again . . . she is so free, so kind . . . entreat her to bind up this broken joint between you and her husband,' Iago urged.

A ray of hope lit up the eyes of Cassio; and Iago saw the thread of his own marvellous web spin on. While Cassio begged Desdemona to repair his fortunes, and she pleaded for him with the Moor, so would Iago pour into Othello's ear the poison that her pleas flowed only from a lust for Cassio. And so would Iago, out of Desdemona's goodness, make the net to enmesh them all . . .

In the garden of the castle the following morning, Cassio spoke to Desdemona. He heard from her own lips that she would give Othello no rest until he restored Cassio to favour; she knew well the lieutenant's loyalty and long-standing, trusted friendship with the Moor.

But seeing Othello himself approaching, and too much ashamed to face him, Cassio hastily took leave of Desdemona and disappeared.

Iago was leading Othello to the garden where he knew this meeting was taking place. He paused, as though surprised to see Cassio there. He let a mutter slither from his lips, 'Ha! I like not that!' just loud enough for Othello half to hear it.

'What do you say?' Othello asked. He waved affectionately to Desdemona. 'Was that not Cassio parted from my wife?'

'Cassio, my lord?' Iago's voice spoke volumes of surprise. 'I cannot think that he would steal away so guilty-like, seeing you coming!'

'I do believe it was he,' Othello assured him, a little puzzled. But the puzzlement was in a moment gone. He stretched his arms, and lifted his face up to feel the balmy air: he was wrapped in such contentment since he had stepped onto this island.

Here he had reached the zenith of his love for Desdemona; no pinnacle could reach higher, no peak could be more perfect than his adoration for this woman who had, against all opposition, chosen him.

She had seen him arrive. True to her promise to Lieutenant Cassio, she at once took up his cause. 'Good, my lord, if I have any grace or power to move you, I beg you, call Cassio back.'

'Not now, sweet Desdemona, some other time,' Othello told her gently, smiling a little at her earnestness.

'But shall it be shortly?' she persisted.

'The sooner, sweet, for you,' he assured her.

'Shall it be tonight, at supper?' she pressed him.

'No, not tonight.'

'Tomorrow then, or Tuesday morn, or Tuesday noon or night. I beg you, name the time, but let it not be longer than three days away.'

Watching her face so fired with her sincerity, Othello felt that he would almost swoon. Her look, the perfume of her skin, her nearness, almost overwhelmed him. So much he loved her now! 'I will deny you *nothing,*' he murmured, and took her in his arms; and she, content with this, withdrew.

'How I do love you,' he whispered after her. 'And when I do not love you, chaos is come again!'

'My noble lord,' Iago broke in upon his thoughts.

'What do you say, Iago?' Othello asked, jovially.

'Did Michael Cassio, when you wooed my lady, know of your love?'

'He did, from first to last: why do you ask?'

'But for the satisfaction of my thought,' and Iago seemed to ponder.

Curiosity stirred mildly in Othello. 'Why of your thought Iago?'

'I did not think he had been acquainted with her,' replied Iago, as though this thought were the slightest morsel in the world.

'Oh yes, and went between us very often,' Othello said.

'Indeed!'

'Indeed!' Othello mimicked him, 'Aye, indeed,' he snorted. What did Iago think that meant? 'Is he not honest?' he teased, knowing the answer without any doubt.

'Honest, my lord!' said Iago, slowly, considering the word.

And so he began: a look, a pause, a question, a smothered exclamation, a sideways slither of his eyes. So did Iago weave, with thread on thread, his web: a pattern, gossamer light at first, of fancies, which touched Othello, quick, at once dismissed, and then returned, for Iago to tease them out . . .

Was Cassio honest? Iago *thought* he was, and men *should* be what they seem . . .

'By heaven, I'll know your thoughts,' Othello cried, for a worm had entered him, a small gnawing worm. Though he knew there was no reason to doubt the honesty of Desdemona, though he knew she loved him passionately and had endured the rejection of her father to follow him, yet now slowly, the worm began to eat its way into his certainties . . .

'Oh, beware, my lord, of jealousy!' Iago burst out as though prompted by a passion stronger than he could master. 'It is the green-eyed monster which mocks the meat it feeds on!'

'Oh misery!' Othello twisted and turned inside, his knowledge of his wife warring with terrors he had never felt before. Though a part of him knew that he must, he could no longer turn away from this vile pattern that Iago spun. He *knew* his wife was honest and that Cassio was honest. Yet he knew also that Iago, this plain-spoken, loyal man was also honest and would not hint such things to tear his soul without good cause!

Then he remembered once again the strength of Desdemona's love, and he felt a surge of faith in her.

'I will not draw the smallest fear or doubt of her,' he told Iago, 'for she had eyes, and she chose me,' and now Othello drew an infinity of strength from this one memory.

'No, Iago,' he declared. 'I'll *see* before I doubt. When I doubt, prove; and on the *proof* away at once with love, or jealousy . . .'

'Look to your wife,' was all Iago said. 'Observe her well with Cassio.' The Moor, he pointed out, being a foreigner to Venetian ways, could not expect to know how well the women of Venice were versed in pranks so well concealed that their duped husbands never knew.

The worm returned, and with it a rotten core of fear eaten by a thousand differences which the Moor felt keenly between himself and all of Venice. *He was not one of them.* And while his reputation and his power had soared across the gap, now it seemed to yawn at him with menacing jaws. And well Iago knew how to touch this tender spot so lightly, yet so painfully.

'I think that Desdemona is honest,' Othello said; but on his face had come a haunted look.

But could Othello not see, Iago said, that Desdemona, having turned away from marriage with men of her own kind, might now repent and look again to *Venetian* men for love?

A great weariness flowed over Othello now, as though he had lost a battle, and it had left him drained on the field. Why had he married? This honest creature, Iago, doubtless saw and knew more, much more than he unfolded . . .

'I am abused,' he said the words he feared to say, half a question, half a statement; and as he said them they took life and became for a moment, true. And they were deadening to him. He gestured Iago away, to leave him to himself. 'My relief must be to loathe her,' he whispered, fearful of the thought.

He heard Desdemona's slight step approaching and there was a rush of blood into his head.

'Oh, if she be false, then heaven mocks itself. I'll not believe it!'

Desdemona saw him press his forehead with some pain, and rushed to him. 'Are you not well?'

'I have a pain upon my foreheard, here,' he muttered, and turned his gaze from her in misery.

'Let me bind it, hard,' she murmured, softly so as not to hurt his head, and wound her handkerchief about his temples.

'It is too little,' Othello brushed it away. And neither saw the handkerchief fall to the ground, nor Iago's wife, Emilia, snatch it up.

It was the Moor's first gift to Desdemona, a delicate tracery of strawberries upon a glorious weave of colour. For some reason which Emilia did not know, Iago had a hundred times asked her to steal it.

Now she had it, and she would swiftly take it to him, to please him.

Othello writhed now upon a wrack, enslaved by images which ripped his dreams and tore his brain, so that he could never sleep, or stop the thoughts: Desdemona was false! His exquisite wife in whom he had vested all the stored-up love of his tempestuous life, toying, *laughing*, behind his back, with his friend, Cassio!

'Villain!' he seized Iago, 'give me proof! If you but slander her and torture me . . . !' he wept, 'I think my wife is honest, and I think that she is not. I think that you are just, and think that you are not . . . I'll have some proof!' he shrieked.

Iago had it. He had heard Cassio talking in his sleep of Desdemona, and urging her to take great care to hide their love from the Moor.

And was there not a handkerchief of Desdemona's, a wisp of cloth spotted with strawberries . . . ?

Othello froze. He hung upon a precipice and looked down into a void . . .

Iago had seen Cassio wipe his beard with it!

Othello plunged. Inside his mind, all certainties collapsed and all was chaos. The noble general who had stood his ground against a thousand foes and stilled the vile outpourings of Brabantio with a single hand, now fell before a tempest of fear and bitterness that swallowed him.

'Within these three days,' he muttered viciously, 'let me hear you say, Iago, that Cassio's not alive.'

'My friend is dead; it is done at your request,' Iago promised. And then the master-stroke:

'But let her live . . .'

'Damn her!' Othello's savage cry heralded the closing of Iago's web. 'Damn her!'

Desdemona fretted at the loss of her much-treasured handkerchief. She kept it always by her, and its disappearance filled her with a nervousness she did not understand. She did not want Othello to find out, for though she had no cause she felt a gathering cloud about them, and it chilled her. Othello behaved so oddly! He would no longer meet her eyes, and yet she could find no cause for it.

She pressed on with her pleas for Cassio, though, for she had promised the good lieutenant that she would; and this, at least, was something she could accomplish in these strange vacant days since Othello had withdrawn from her.

But Othello had a single answer when she spoke of Michael Cassio. He asked her for the handkerchief. He said he had a cold . . .

She saw at once he knew she did not have it.

'Is it lost? Speak!' he cried, and his voice was thunder in her ears.

'It is not lost!' she grew confused, 'but what if it were?'

'Fetch it,' he stormed. 'Let me see it.'

Desdemona flinched. 'Why so I can, sir. But I will not now. This is a trick to put me from my pleas for Cassio! Pray you, let Cassio be received again. Talk to me of Cassio,' she said again, as though her fate had locked itself to this one name, and she could not let go.

'Away!' bellowed Othello, and thrust her from him. Damned by her own tongue! And he rushed away from his bewildered wife who shrank in terror from this creature of spitting fury. This was not the man that she had married! He was transformed beyond all understanding.

There was a woman of the island named Bianca, who doted on Cassio and dogged his footsteps everywhere. Now she waylaid him again.

Cassio had come to find out whether Desdemona's pleas for him were having any success, and he was anxious for Bianca to leave. He produced a task for her to do for him: to take a handkerchief which he had found lying in his room, and copy the design on it. Though he did not know where the cloth had come from, yet he liked it very much . . .

So fast the blows now fell on Othello's mind, that he could no longer hold them all. He trembled, muttered, stumbled, shrieked disjointed

words, and when, before Iago's watchful eyes, he fell into a foaming
trance, Iago's ecstasy knew no bounds. 'Work on, my medicine, work!'
he breathed. Truly the Moor's mind was breaking apart, and the end
must be in sight!

The Moor was gaining consciousness again: confused, and babbling
of blood. Quickly Iago whispered in his ear that Cassio was hereabouts
and if he hid, he would hear the man damned from his own mouth.

Out of Othello's earshot, he asked Cassio about Bianca. Cassio always
laughed whenever this lady's name was mentioned, to think how the
woman hunted him and he told several merry tales about her.

Othello heard only the tales; he heard Cassio talking of a woman's
lustful love, and believed that Cassio spoke of Desdemona. He saw
Bianca shout at Cassio, and throw a wisp of strawberry-spotted cloth at
him, angry that it was a love-token from another woman.

His gaze now rested on the handkerchief, on his love for Desdemona,
flung down in contempt and left to flutter on the ground.

'Aye, let her rot,' he felt the rage swell up inside his head. 'Let her rot, and perish, and be damned tonight; for she shall not live!'

His faithful ensign had returned to him now that he had drawn the final proof from Cassio's lips.

'Get me some poison, Iago; this night; this night, Iago!'

'Do it not with poison,' Iago told him softly. 'Strangle her in bed!'

Lodovico, a kinsman of Desdemona's, came from Venice bringing messages for Othello. The Moor, he noticed, met him with a distracted air; and while Desdemona gave him a gracious welcome, her face was strangely pale, and her eyes flickered nervously towards Othello. She spoke of some division between Cassio and her husband which she hoped to heal. Othello seemed to read the letters from the Duke with only half an eye, and was more given to casting vicious glances at his wife and hissing at every word of Cassio.

The letters commanded Othello to return to Venice and leave the government of Cyprus to Cassio. To the Venetian Senate, this was merely because Othello's mission here in Cyprus was now done, and he was needed for other tasks.

But to Othello, this recall from Cyprus seemed to turn, all in a piece with the deceit by Cassio and his wife.

'Devil!' he shrieked suddenly, and struck her full across the face, the red weal of his hand gleaming like a streak of blood across her cheek.

'My lord,' gasped Lodovico, 'this would not be believed in Venice!'

'Devil! Devil! Out of my sight!' was all the answer Othello gave, his face contorted with disgust.

'I will not stay to offend you,' Desdemona whispered through hopeless tears, and backed away. Othello, muttering insults, pursued her off. Lodovico watched the scene with disbelief. Was this the noble Moor believed by Venice's full Senate to be sufficient in all things? Was this the nature that passion could not shake?

'He is much changed,' Iago acknowledged regretfully.

'Are his wits safe? Is he not light of brain? To strike his wife!' Lodovico wondered.

'If only,' Iago murmured softly to him, 'If only I knew that stroke would prove the worst!'

Othello sent for Desdemona. 'What are you?' he demanded.

'Your wife, my lord,' she said. 'Your true and loyal wife.'

'Come, swear it. Damn yourself,' he hissed. 'Be double-damned, swear you are honest, for heaven truly knows you are as false as hell!'

'To whom, my lord? With whom? How am I false?' she begged. She despaired. She languished in a hopelessness that deadened her . . . She had no words to speak of this, no further answer for her transformed lord. She seemed to Emilia to be almost asleep.

She asked Emilia to lay her wedding sheets upon the bed that night.

Roderigo was impatient with affairs in Cyprus. He had plied Iago with a wealth of gold and jewels for Desdemona, but she had not sent for him! Slowly, he had begun to wonder if he was deceived. But he was ready to go to Desdemona and demand his gifts returned!

Iago was ready to reveal the next stage of his scheme: if Roderigo would show his strength of purpose this night – the very next he would have Desdemona! Did Roderigo know that Cassio had been given command in Cyprus, and that Othello and Desdemona were being sent to Mauritania?

If Cassio were removed, Othello would have to stay in Cyprus. Only this could prevent the disappearance of Roderigo's love far beyond his grasp. Cassio *must* be killed. Swiftly Iago sketched out exactly how . . .

Desdemona waited for Othello. He had commanded her to dismiss Emilia and go to bed and she was anxious not to offend him further.

A shiver fluttered through her, an ache for the lost warmth of adoration, so richly won, so quickly gone from her beloved husband. Would it return again? She was afraid, and the fear was great, though she could find no words for it. Her eyes fell on the bridal sheets Emilia had laid on the bed.

'If I do die,' she whispered, involuntarily, 'shroud me in one of those same sheets.'

'Come, come,' Emilia chided her. And yet the coldness had touched her heart too, and she jumped at shadows . . .

A dark street near the harbour; whispers and shufflings; a shape that melted away and left another huddled against the wall. It was Roderigo, now fully primed by Iago, waiting by Bianca's door for Cassio to leave.

Iago stood aside and watched. It mattered not at all to him who killed who, for now he needed both to die. Roderigo bleated for his jewels,

and would soon begin to talk to others . . .

It was quickly done. Cassio's confident step; a stab from Roderigo's dagger, and from the hidden Iago a cut into Cassio's leg.

Lodovico, making his way with others to his ship, heard loud groans. He searched, and saw Iago running to the scene holding a light. Together they discovered wounded Cassio on the ground, alive, but white with loss of blood, and there Roderigo, stabbed by Cassio.

Under cover of the dark, Iago thrust his dagger hard into Roderigo, who in the moment of his death saw the true colours of his friend for the first and only time. But Roderigo's mouth was stopped, and Iago, riding high on such success, knew that on this night his grand design would reach its perfect peak.

Desdemona lay between the bridal sheets, below a lamp. She lay quite motionless, as though she waited even in her sleep.

Othello moved towards her. He walked in a dream. All rage was stilled, all anger cold. Only a single purpose moved him on, and in a trance he glided to it, murmuring, his thoughts and fears and horrors circling ever in his head.

'Yet I'll not shed her blood,' he whispered, 'nor scar that skin of hers, whiter than snow . . . Yet she must die, else she'll betray more men.' The thought no longer held its fire for him, as though his memory spoke of a task once given him, not yet accomplished.

He looked up at the lamp. 'Put out the light.' Then he looked down at her soft face upon the pillow. 'And then put out the light.' But once the light of Desdemona was put out, it could not be rekindled.

He bowed across her, and felt her breath caress his face, a warm, balmy breath that almost caught him in the wonder of his love again.

She stirred, and woke, and saw Othello leaning over her, his eyes a deadening mask of darkness.

'Have you prayed tonight, Desdemona? I would not kill your unprepared spirit.'

'Talk you of killing?' she gasped.

'Aye, I do.'

She shrank within the bed. His lowering face, his grim monotony of tone, froze her. Like a child that fears in innocence and does not understand escape, she cringed before the final stroke. And then, as though he could not leave the thought alone, he cried, 'That handkerchief, which I so loved and gave you, you gave to Cassio!'

'No, by my life and soul! Send for the man and ask him!'

'Sweet soul,' he intoned now without emotion. 'Take heed, take heed of lying. You are on your deathbed.'

'I never did offend you in my life. I never gave Cassio tokens of love!'

'He has confessed.'

'He will not say so!'

'No.' The word was final. 'His mouth is stopped.'

Desdemona sank into the pillows. 'He is betrayed, and I undone,' she said. And with these little words she signed the final testimony of guilt for her avenging husband. All pleas of innocence abandoned, she begged desperately for life.

'It is too late,' he said.

He lifted the pillow from the bed, and pressed it on her face, and held it there until all breath of life was stilled.

He kneeled above the deed, and seemed not to know how long the minutes were that passed between the flight of Desdemona's life and the wild knocking at the door which roused him from his trance.

In pure whiteness, shrouded in the bridal sheets, his wife lay dead before him. Emilia's knocks broke in upon him. He got up and started for the door, forgot, turned back, stood near the bed, remembered the knock again, remembered the bed, and drew the curtains round it; and went now to open the door.

As Emilia rushed in, there was a sudden gasp of fleeting life from Desdemona. 'Falsely, falsely murdered!'

Emilia wrenched the curtains back and tried to rouse her.

'A guiltless death I die,' the words fell from her paling lips.

'Who has done this?' Emilia wept.

'Nobody, I myself. Farewell,' and Desdemona died.

'She's like a liar gone to burning hell,' Othello screamed. 'It was I that killed her!'

'The more angel she, and you the blacker devil!' Emilia rounded on him. In disbelief she heard him spit his accusations: Desdemona false, Desdemona locked in lust with Cassio! 'Your husband knew it all!'

Emilia stopped. She heard the words again. *Husband*. She repeated it. Once, twice, a third time. And suddenly she saw the web her husband spun, and understood.

She shrieked for help. They came rushing to her cries, and broke in upon the dreadful scene: Montano, Ludovico, others; and Iago, hot to see his work.

But he had left one stroke of his design imperfect. He had not seen how his wife loved Desdemona. And now this love would not be stilled, for him or anyone! Desdemona false, she shouted. It was a vicious lie!

A light began to dawn in Othello's mangled mind. But yet it had to fight the darkness of Iago's poison.

'The handkerchief,' he whispered. 'The handkerchief.'

And then Emilia truly understood. And as she turned, her face aflame with knowledge of her husband's evil, Iago saw his end in sight. He rushed at her and drove his dagger hard into her heart, and fled.

Now Othello knew, as well. He saw Desdemona dead, and understood what he had done. He felt the web of lies which spun its tissues round and through his mind, silencing his judgement, and killing his humanity. He had become that savage thing that Iago always wanted him to be . . .

They caught Iago and dragged him back. Othello reeled at the sight of him. He stumbled towards his ensign and with a sudden cry of pitiful rage, he plunged his sword into him.

Iago regarded him in silence. Though his scheme was all exposed and he was finished, yet how perfect was the downfall of the Moor! Gone was all nobility, all honour, greatness, wisdom; here was this creature who had killed an innocent upon a villain's word.

'I bleed, sir,' he taunted, 'but not killed.'

'Will you demand that demi-devil why he has ensnared my soul and body?' Othello whispered.

'Demand me nothing. What you know, you know. From this time forth I never will speak word,' Iago sneered.

Lodovico addressed the Moor. 'You must foresake this room and go with us. Your power and your command are taken over and Cassio rules in Cyprus. You shall remain a prisoner till the nature of your fault is known to the Venetian state . . .'

Othello stood once more quite still and calm, as once he had. He moved towards the bed where Desdemona lay. For a long, silent moment, he gazed at her.

'Soft you: a word or two before you go,' he murmured to the assembled Venetians. 'I have done the state some service, and they know it. I pray you, in your letters, when you relate these unlucky deeds, speak of me as I am . . . then must you speak of one that loved not wisely, but too well; of one not easily jealous, but being wrought, perplexed in the extreme; of one whose hand threw a pearl away . . .' He paused and in his eyes there was a gleam of secret knowledge. 'And say besides, that in Aleppo once, where a malignant Turk beat a Venetian and betrayed the state, I took the dog by the throat . . .'

Before their eyes could catch his action or their hands could fly to stop him, he slid a secret dagger from his robes, 'and struck him, thus!' he cried, and thrust the dagger in his breast.

He spoke only to Desdemona now, so soft it was a whisper on the wind, his lips caressing hers . . . 'I kissed you before I killed you; no way but this; killing myself, to die upon a kiss.'

So ended the tale of Othello, Moor of Venice. It was the tale of Iago, too, whose work had reached its zenith in this night of savagery, and from whose sealed lips never spilled the reason for his villainy.

Hamlet

High on the towers of Elsinore, royal castle to the kings of Denmark, three men met in the bitter winds of a chill night, while far below them an angry sea crashed and pounded at the rocks. But it was not that booming menace, nor the midnight gloom that kept them close together, searching the darkness with wary eyes.

'What, has this thing appeared again tonight?' Marcellus asked Bernardo, his fellow Officer of the Watch.

'I have seen nothing,' Bernardo answered him, and looked beyond Marcellus, uneasily. While their friend, Horatio, leaned on the parapet and watched the turbulent sea below.

'Horatio says it is our fantasy, and will not let belief take hold of him,' Marcellus told Bernardo, stamping his feet and blowing on his icy hands. 'So I've asked him along to watch. If the apparition comes . . .'

'Tush, tush, it will not appear,' Horatio shook his head at them, half-smiling at their nervousness. He tugged his cloak about him, hunching his shoulders against the wind. Their tale could certainly not be believed: a ghostly figure stalking the battlements by night! This strange story had been almost the only greeting from his anxious friends on his arrival here in Elsinore from Wittenberg.

Yet he could understand how this dark platform, suspended above a raging sea, could plant such tremors even in a soldier's mind. So bitter cold it was! So bleak and comfortless!

'Look!' The sudden cry of Marcellus sliced at the darkness and spun Horatio round. 'Look where it comes again!'

'Just like the king that's dead!' Bernardo whispered across the quivering silence that had dropped about the towers.

Horatio looked where his finger pointed, but saw only a mist that curled across the battlements towards them . . .

And then, he looked again. All certainty was numbed, all understanding fled, for through the icy curtain a looming figure moved. It trod the swirling mists with soundless march: no clink of metal or scrape of boot on stone; only the great figure's slow, silent, majestic tread. As it neared, it turned its face towards them, and in horror they shrank back for what a sorrow swelled within that bloodless face!

Bernardo seized Horatio's arm. 'Does it not look just like the king?'

For a long moment Horatio could not speak.

'Most like,' he whispered, then. 'It fills me with fear and wonder.'

'It wants to be spoken to,' Bernardo said.

'Question it, Horatio,' urged Marcellus. Horatio shook off the numbing fear and raised his voice with loud determination.

'What are you? By heaven, speak!' But as his voice echoed across the battlements, the ghostly figure turned in the mists and moved away.

'Stay! Speak, speak!' Horatio cried after it.

But it was gone. Trembling and pale he stood there. This was surely something more than fantasy!

And what did it mean? That face and form so like the king; so noble, fine and strong in life, now coming to them in death all lacerated with an inward grief and filled with welling sorrows. Did it foretell some dreadful menace to the state of Denmark?

He thought then of his friend, Hamlet, the young Prince of Denmark, and beloved son of this dead king whose ghost now stalked the battlements. Prince Hamlet *must* be told of this. Surely his father, even dead, would bare his sorrows to his son!

This the three men agreed, in solemn secrecy: Prince Hamlet must be told. This very night he would be brought to see this terrifying thing.

Even as their minds still reeled with the apparition of a king now dead, the new king, jovial and very much alive, performed the duties of a monarch with lordly hand and flowing words in halls festooned with the rich glitter of pomp and celebration.

This new king, Claudius, was brother to the king that had just died, and he had cause to celebrate more than his ascent to the throne of Denmark. Swiftly following his coronation as the king, Claudius had married the dead king's wife.

So Elsinore was not in mourning for the passing of a king. Instead the gaudy brilliance of velvets, silks and jewels decked out the courtiers who fluttered among silken hangings and heady flowers while feasting,

drinking, music, dance and song trumpeted the gaiety of wedding celebrations. All the world, it seemed, applauded the happy event.

All, that is, except Prince Hamlet. Hamlet loved his father with a fierce pride and a passion that could not be so sharply stopped by death. He loved his mother too. And he had thought she was the most loving wife his noble father could have had. How she had hung upon his father's words and deeds, as though she drew her life from his! How her adoration seemed to grow with every minute!

And now? What now? That noble father dead: not even two months dead. It seemed as if it was only yesterday his majestic form had graced these halls . . . And what of his mother, this loving wife? This passionate, devoted wife had wed again! Within a month! This wife had wed her husband's brother! Wed! Against all the customs of the land, which frowned upon a marriage to a husband's brother and called it *incest*.

Wed! To a man as foul and odious and mean as his great father had been glorious.

How was it that the world applauded it? How was it that he, Hamlet, was the only one to feel the poisoning dishonour of his mother's marriage and ache with its treachery to his beloved father?

And so he shrank within his dark mourning clothes as if he would recede from view and melt away, forever escaping these garish, gaudy, rotten halls. Yet he watched the king, his uncle, whose smile was as wide as his broad, bloated face and whose hand never left its firm possession of the jewelled fingers of his queen. And Hamlet felt a loathing for the very ground on which they stood: his whole body was consumed with longing for his father; misery and loneliness wrapped him in a pain without end.

'But now my nephew Hamlet and my son,' King Claudius, all glowing smiles, was now approaching him. 'How is it that the clouds still hang on you?'

'Good Hamlet,' his mother added her pleas. 'Cast away your gloom and look like a friend on Claudius.' She smiled luxuriously at her husband and put her other hand on his, then turned to her son again. 'Do not for ever seek your noble father in the dust; you know death is common: all that lives must die . . .'

Hamlet saw her as in a mist that let through only that smiling, smiling face. Was this his mother, who could say such words? Five words! So was a king dismissed, a husband gone! All that lives must die, she said!

'Aye, madam, death is common,' he said bitterly.

'If it be so,' she pressed on, refusing to understand his tone, 'why does it seem so heavy a grief with you?'

A sudden heat filled up his brain and fired the dark chill within into a smouldering flame.

'Seem, madam!' he cried with scorn. 'No, it *is*; I do not know "*seem*". It is not alone my inky cloak, good mother, nor suits of solemn black, nor sighs, nor cries, nor the sad expression of my face that show me for what I am.' He turned away, feeling the tears that burst within.

With an impatient sweep of his glittering hand, the king interrupted him. 'It is sweet and commendable in your nature, Hamlet, to give these mourning duties to your father. But you must know, your father lost a father; that father lost, lost his . . . We pray you, cast aside this sorrow, and think of me as of a father.' He softened his voice and urged a warmth into it, 'And as for your intention in going back to study in Wittenberg, it is most strongly against our desire. We beseech you to remain here, in the cheer and comfort of our eye, our chief courtier, nephew and our son.'

The queen nodded and tilted her handsome head, and smiled as if she could simply smile and nod away his misery.

What did it matter? What did anything matter to him in this looming emptiness that entered his world again and doused the fire of anger. Elsinore, or Wittenberg, it was all the same. 'I shall in all my best obey you, madam,' he muttered, and turned away from her.

He watched them go, this gilded queen and king, wafted in a cloud of courtiers who fluttered like desperate butterflies about an overblown flower. The silence settled about him. But there was no peace in it, only a gloom that shut out all sunlight.

He wished that he could simply cease to be, to end his life now, and so end all the pain.

'Oh that this too, too solid flesh would melt, thaw and resolve itself into a dew!' he cried into the void around him. 'Oh God! God! How weary, stale, flat and unprofitable seem to me all the uses of this world. It's an unweeded garden that grows to seed . . . things rank and gross in nature possess it!' And what a stench and ugliness was in it!

He saw his father's face again, as he had been in life, and in his mind he traced the contours of his strong, wise face. Only two month's dead! So excellent a king.' And then with sudden horror he remembered his uncle's face, bloated with drink and larded with that gleam of cunning.

'Heaven and earth! A beast would have mourned longer! It is not, and it cannot come to good. But break, my heart, for I must hold my tongue!' A sudden noise behind him whirled him round. He saw three men approaching, and hastened to answer their greeting as courteously as he could before moving away.

And then a beam of sun broke through his clouds: he saw the man who spoke was no twittering courtier from Elsinore but Horatio, dear Horatio, his great friend from university in Wittenberg! Here was a man whose honest friendship was as dear to him as any he had ever had!

But why in Elsinore? He grasped his friend's hand eagerly, and urged an explanation.

'My lord,' replied Horatio, unwillingly. 'I came to see your father's funeral.'

Hamlet regarded him with a long, silent look that chilled Horatio as surely as the sight of Hamlet's father's ghost.

'I pray you, do not mock me, fellow-student,' Hamlet said, 'I think it was to see my mother's wedding.'

'Indeed, my lord, it followed hard upon it,' Horatio answered.

'Thrift, thrift, Horatio!' he said, sarcasm heavy in his voice 'The funeral-baked meats did coldly furnish forth the marriage tables! I would rather have met my greatest enemy in heaven than ever see that day, Horatio!'

Horatio told him then, carefully and with precise attention to the exact events, what they had witnessed on the battlements.

With each word of their extraordinary tale, a flame seemed to flicker across Prince Hamlet's face, as though a hidden life was kindling there again. With sudden resolution he said, 'I will watch tonight. Perhaps it will walk again. If it looks like my noble father I'll speak to it, though hell itself should open and bid me hold my peace!'

Warmly he grasped their hands. 'Farewell. Upon the battlements, between eleven and twelve, I'll visit you.'

His father's spirit! He *would* speak to it! It seemed almost as though this phantom was an echo of the sombre misery within his soul, almost as though some dreadful knowledge was struggling upward from the kingdom of the dead towards him.

'Foul deeds will rise,' he murmured with an inward shiver of dread, 'though all the earth may bury them from men's eyes.'

The Lord Chamberlain in Claudius' Court was one Polonius, an elderly gentleman with many years of politics behind him and a high opinion of the skills and infinite wisdom he had learned in such a wily world. The ebb and flow of power, its cut and thrust and counter-thrust was his life-blood; the schemes, manoeuvres, plans and strategies of courtly government were all his daily bread.

He had a son, Laertes, a handsome youth with boundless energy and a well-cultivated love of all the pleasures in life. From Paris (a most fitting place of residence for a man of fashion) Laertes had come to see King Claudius' coronation. Now he was leaving Elsinore again.

Polonius also had a daughter, Ophelia. She was a gentle, pretty girl to whom the world had shown no harshness or cruelty. She bore no wounds or bruises on her simple, modest nature and so she felt only a limitless trust and love for those who loved and cared for her: her brother Laertes, her father Polonius, and Prince Hamlet, who had in recent months most warmly vowed his love for her.

So, as Laertes prepared to leave for France, these children of Polonius said their affectionate farewells and Laertes took the opportunity to give his sister the benefit of all his worldly knowledge concerning the weaknesses of men. Ophelia listened to her brother's words with fond attention. She should (he said) not take Prince Hamlet's words of love too seriously. They were no more than the warm words of youth: they would be sweet, not lasting.

'His will is not his own,' he asserted, confidently, 'for on a prince's choice depends the safety and the health of the whole state.'

His sister smiled a little teasingly at him. Of course she understood the wisdom in all he said. But she knew also the warmth of love that flowed to her from Hamlet; she understood that too.

The portly figure of their father bustled in. 'Still here, Laertes! Aboard, aboard, for shame! There, my blessing go with you,' and with that he let forth a tumbling stream of warnings: solemn comparisons of good and bad, of friends and enemies, of cost and gain, learnt (as Polonius believed) in the vast storehouse of his experience.

Laertes listened with all the attention of a dutiful son, then held his hand out to his sister. 'Farewell, Ophelia; and remember well what I have said to you.'

'It is locked in my memory and you yourself shall keep the key of it,' Ophelia assured him, warmly returning his embrace.

At once suspicious of a conversation which he had not heard, Polonius peered at his daughter with narrowed eyes.

'What is it he has said to you?'

Ophelia blushed and lowered her gaze.

'Something concerning Prince Hamlet,' she replied.

Ah! Polonius smiled grimly to himself. Something was brewing here!

He put his hand beneath his daughter's chin and tilted her face up so that his eyes could peer deep within and winkle out the secret.

'What is between you? Give me up the truth!'

'He has, my lord, made many tenders of his affection to me,' Ophelia declared with quiet pride.

'Affection!' Polonius dismissed the word with a single wave of his wrinkled hand. 'Pooh! You speak like a green girl!'

'My lord, he told me of his love in honourable fashion,' Ophelia protested indignantly.

He caught her arm impatiently. Clearly this daughter of his had no sense at all concerning the ways of the world and particularly of men! Surely she, so much beneath a prince's station in life, could not take a prince's words of love as meaning anything! He smelt a scandal brewing here! If he did not take care Ophelia would disgrace herself and her own father, making a pretty fool of him!

'I would not, from this time forth, have you talk with Prince Hamlet,' he warned her. 'Look to it, I charge you.' He wagged his finger in her face and his tone defied any disobedience.

Ophelia stared at his wagging finger with shocked disbelief. Why did they all believe that Hamlet's words of love were false? Why were they all so certain that he was not honest and merely played with her?

She knew Hamlet, in her heart, and knew he was an honest, loving man, who would not trifle with her love.

Yet she remembered her brother's warning words. Did not her brother and her father love her too? Did they not seek to protect her from all harm? With their greater understanding of the world, perhaps they *did* know more of this than she . . . perhaps . . .

She sighed, and fought back the pricking tears. Perhaps . . .

She bowed her head before her father's piercing gaze.

'I will obey, my lord,' she said.

Horatio and Marcellus waited with Hamlet on the battlements. There was no wind tonight, and through the still, cold air the blare of trumpets and the boisterous boom of cannon reached their ears. With heavy heart Hamlet listened to the raucous sounds which were the braying accompaniments to the revelry of the king.

What a blot upon the name of Denmark, this drinking and revelry through day and night! Was this the only mark of the royal house of Denmark: its king and courtiers could drink all men under the table?

'Look!' Horatio stopped him. 'Look, my lord, it comes.'

'Angels and ministers of grace defend us!' Hamlet leapt to his feet and stared, finding no other words to pass his trembling lips.

And then he seemed to haul on inner strength and took a step towards the phantom. 'I will speak to you: I'll call you king, father, royal Dane. Oh answer me! What does this mean? What should we do?'

Before their spell-bound eyes the phantom's hand rose through the mists and hovered. Then slowly it beckoned to Prince Hamlet: once, twice, three times there came that slow, pleading motion of the hand.

As if drawn by an invisible thread, Hamlet moved after it.

'Do not go with it,' Marcellus warned.

'Do not, my lord,' Horatio said, and held Hamlet tightly by the arm.

'Why?' Hamlet cried. 'What should I fear? I do not value my life above the price of a pin! It waves me forth again. I'll follow it!'

'You shall not go, my lord,' Marcellus grasped his shoulder.

'Be ruled,' Horatio spoke gently to his friend. 'You shall not go.'

'My fate cries out! Unhand me gentlemen. By heaven I'll make a ghost of him that stops me!' And with a burst of strength Hamlet threw off their hold and rushed into the swirling mists.

Horatio stared after him. What was going to come of this? He felt the chill of doom across his heart: for Hamlet, and for all of them.

Marcellus said quietly, 'Come, let's follow him. It is not right to leave him alone with this.' And with a deep shudder of dread, he added, 'Something is rotten in the state of Denmark.'

Father and son now stood together, wrapped in the silent blanket of the night and in their lonely grief.

'Mark me,' the apparition stared with longing across the boundary of death that kept him from his son. 'My hour is almost come.'

'Speak,' Hamlet whispered. 'I am bound to hear.'

'If ever you did love your father,' the spirit's voice welled from the castle stones and echoed in the air.

'Revenge his foul and most unnatural murder!'

Murder! The word boomed across the towers and blasted into Hamlet as if it would hurl him in a thousand shattered pieces across the earth.

'*Murder!*'

'Murder most foul,' the echo of his father's voice tore through his ears.

Murder! But all the world knew that his father died from a serpent's poisoned sting!

'Know now,' the spirit breathed, 'the serpent that did sting your father's life now wears his crown.'

'My uncle!' Numbly Hamlet looked into his father's bloodless, anguished face. Numbly he struggled to hear him through the hammering in his brain: how Claudius had crept to where the king slept peacefully in his orchard; how Claudius had poured a poison in his ear that coursed through his veins like quicksilver and soured his life.

But now a new horror crept from the phantom's lips into Hamlet's mind, and held him, stunned, beneath its weight: his mother, who had seemed to love his father so, had, *even before his father's death* entwined herself with that foul, murderous Claudius' lust.

Hamlet swayed in an agony of shock. A mother not merely rushing to wed too soon after a father's death, but a mother steeped in dishonesty and faithlessness even while his father was still alive!

'Thus was I, sleeping, by a brother's hand of life, of crown, of queen, at once dispatched,' the spirit mourned. 'If you have nature in you, do not bear it. Let not the royal bed be a couch for damned incest!'

Now the darkness had begun to pale and the scent of morning spiced the air. With a long and lingering gaze, the spirit looked into his son's stricken face.

'Farewell! Farewell! Hamlet, *remember me!*' And as the dawn crept hesitantly across the hill, the phantom faded.

Hamlet was alone. 'Hold, hold, my heart,' he whispered, swaying, as though he would fall to the icy stones and never rise again.

'Remember you!' He fought to hold his staggering brain together.

He *would* remember! He would wipe away all else his memory held and this commandment alone would live within his brain: Revenge his father's foul and most unnatural murder! In his mind's eye he saw his mother's face as she had turned her gaze on smiling Claudius. 'Oh most vile woman!' he cried. 'Oh villain, villain; smiling, damned villain!'

With a burst of energy he pulled a notebook from his pocket and scribbled passionately on it as though by writing he would purge the agony from within himself and stamp it forever on the paper. 'One may smile, and smile, and be a villain. At least I'm sure it may be so in Denmark; so, uncle, there you are.' He snapped the notebook closed.

Now his head was clearer. He drew a deep breath. Revenge. He had sworn it. *Revenge*. As from a great distance, he heard the frantic cries of his friends still searching for him. He steeled himself to meet their questioning eyes, for how could he tell this tale? How could such evil be believed by honest men? He hailed them now, and swiftly hid his knowledge deep within, preparing to fend off their anxious questions from behind a shield of bitter jokes.

'How is it, my noble lord?' Marcellus reached him first.

'What news, my lord?' Horatio panted, close behind.

'There's never a villain dwelling in all Denmark but he's a crooked man,' Hamlet answered solemnly.

'There needs no ghost, my lord, come from the grave, to tell us this.' Horatio chided him. 'These are but wild and whirling words.'

'I'm sorry if they offend you,' Hamlet replied. But still he jumped from their questions and juggled frantically about their ears with words that told them nothing.

'But this is wondrous strange,' Horatio exclaimed, his unease deepening at this wild, desperate flippancy in his friend.

'There are more things in heaven and earth, Horatio, than are dreamt of in your philosophy,' retorted Hamlet, his unnatural excitement sharpening his tone to him. But already there was the glimmering of a half-formed plan inside his head. Swiftly he urged his friends to keep the secret of this night's mysteries. And then he made them swear another, stranger oath: that, however oddly he might behave in times to come, *even if he seemed a little mad*, they must never, for a moment, hint that they had any knowledge to explain his acts.

They swore. And with his arms about their shoulders Hamlet ushered them out of the darkness of the towers into the castle. But even as he did a brooding gloom began to creep across his heart, threatening to ice the flame of vengeance; for what was this world of murder, treachery, adultery, incest and revenge? It was not his world. This was not the stuff that he was made of!

'The time is out of joint,' he cried inwardly. 'Oh cursed spite, that ever I was born to set it right!'

Two months had passed since that dark night. Laertes, in Paris, was far from his father's watchful eye. Too far, the old Polonius thought, and quickly despatched a spy to snoop about.

Now daughter Ophelia claimed his attention.

'Oh my lord,' she wept, 'I have been so frightened! As I was sewing in my room, Lord Hamlet . . .' she faltered, remembering. This noble prince, this fine, fine man . . . his clothes all crumpled and awry, and with a look so pale and pitiful as if he had been loosed out of hell to tell of its horror . . . 'Hamlet comes before me,' she stuttered.

'Mad for your love?' Polonius questioned eagerly, his mind already racing with what uses he could make of it.

'My lord, I do not know, but truly I do fear it,' answered the bewildered girl. How Hamlet had gazed at her, a long, searching look, as if he would draw each line and contour of her face! 'At last,' she sobbed, 'with a little shaking of my arm, he raised a sigh so piteous and profound as if it would shatter all his bulk and end his being.'

Polonius pulled her quickly from the room. What news he had for the king! This must be the very ecstasy of love, and surely *this* was the source of the madness afflicting the prince these past two months!

'What?' he questioned Ophelia as he hauled her stumbling figure across the halls. 'Have you given him any hard words of late?'

'No, my good lord,' Ophelia struggled to keep up with him. 'But, as you did command, I did repel his letters and denied his access to me.'

'That has made him mad.' For a moment Polonius felt a twinge of sorrow. Perhaps he should have paid more attention to his daughter. But no matter, he had been certain Hamlet only played with her, and he could not possibly risk a scandal that would damage his own reputation at the Court. At least now something could be done.

'Come,' he tugged at Ophelia's hand. 'Let us go to the king.'

But King Claudius and his queen already had plans afoot to sniff out the cause of Hamlet's antics in the past two months. Neither his appearance nor the inward man seemed to resemble what it used to be.

Horatio would shed no light on the reasons for this transformation. So instead the king had sent for two of Hamlet's old school friends, Rosencrantz and Guildenstern. Perhaps these companions of Hamlet's happy youth would find the reason for his melancholy strangeness. This, at any rate was the plan which Claudius put before them, to which the queen added her pleas for help. She did not like to see her son so changed. His continuing unhappiness and growing madness marred the pleasure of her days and too often pierced the warm comforts of her luxurious life. So Rosencrantz and Guildenstern were sent to look for Hamlet and inform the king and queen of all they knew.

It was now that Polonius bustled in, all puffed with pride that he, of all, had found the cause of Hamlet's lunacy. So much he burst to tell it, that the words came spilling like tripping idiots off his tongue.

'To expostulate,' he declared, 'what majesty should be, what duty is, what day is day, night night and time is time . . .'

The queen sighed heavily. How tedious this councillor could be! 'More matter with less art,' she told him.

Polonius bowed, but scarcely paused in the tumbling gambol of his words. 'Your noble son is mad. Consider,' he gazed about him with pleasure at the effect his next pronouncement would have, 'I have a daughter, who in obedience has given me this,' and with a flourish he took a letter from his robes, reading it out with flowing roundness to the words of love, pausing nevertheless to criticize each phrase and so make sure that all his listeners could see his breadth of knowledge.

'Is this letter from Hamlet to Ophelia?' the queen interrupted him.

It was, and now Polonius produced the conclusion of his tale as though it was a rabbit from a conjurer's hat: 'Lord Hamlet, repulsed, fell into a sadness, then into a weakness, and so into the madness in which he raves and we all mourn for.'

'Do you think it is this?' Claudius asked the queen, doubtfully.

'It may be, very likely,' the queen said.

Polonius bustled forward with a little scheme to test the truth of it. He would have Ophelia meet Hamlet, as if by chance, while Polonius and the king could hide nearby and watch how Hamlet behaved to her.

'We will try it,' Claudius said. Of one thing, he was certain. Everything must be done to sniff this matter out. Each day his misgivings about Prince Hamlet were growing. There was no form to his suspicions, just a pricking sense of danger nearing . . .

Even as they hatched the plot, Prince Hamlet himself approached. Polonius urged the royal pair to go, so he could ambush the prince.

'Do you know me, my lord?' Polonius asked Hamlet, preparing to enjoy the encounter.

Hamlet looked up from his book; a brief, vacant stare, and down again. 'Excellent well, you are a fishmonger,' he said.

'Not I, my lord,' Polonius assured him.

'Then I wish you were so honest a man,' Hamlet retorted.

'Honest, my lord!'

'Aye, sir,' Hamlet replied. 'To be honest, as this world goes, is to be one man picked out of ten thousand.'

'That's very true, my lord,' Polonius said, less certain now that he knew quite where this conversation was going.

'Have you a daughter?' Hamlet demanded.

'I have, my lord.'

'Let her not walk in the sun.' Hamlet eyed him solemnly, and returned to the pages of his book.

Still harping on my daughter! Polonius rejoiced. 'He said I was a fishmonger. He is far gone, far gone!' The old man's eyes grew misty thinking of times long past when, in his youth, he too had suffered like this for love. 'What do you read, my lord?' he accosted Hamlet again.

'Words, words, words,' Hamlet held the book up.

'What is the matter, my lord?' Polonius persisted.

'Between who?' Hamlet asked.

'I mean the matter that you read, my lord,' explained Polonius, patiently, as to a very little child.

'Lies, sir,' replied Hamlet, with a gleam in his eye, 'for the rogue says here that old men have grey beards, that their faces are wrinkled . . .'

Polonius stepped back, uncertainly. Though this be madness, yet he could see that there was method in it! He straightened his robes importantly. 'My honourable Lord,' he pronounced, 'I will most humbly take my leave of you.'

Hamlet watched the old man bustle out. What a tedious fool this revered old courtier is, he thought, and how he deserves his place of power in the murky shadow of King Claudius!

He did not see the two men entering the room. Closer to him, he recognized two well-known faces from long-lost, happier days.

'My excellent good friends!' he exclaimed, surprised. 'How do you,

Guildenstern. Ah, Rosencrantz! Good lads, how do you both?' He shook their hands heartily. 'But what have you deserved at the hands of Fortune that she sends you to prison here?'

'Prison, my lord?' exclaimed Guildenstern.

'Denmark's a prison,' Hamlet assured him, 'to me it is a prison.'

'Why then your ambition makes it one,' said Rosencrantz.

Like ice the comment dropped across the easy banter of their words. Hamlet eyed them curiously. Exactly *why* had they come to Elsinore?

'Were you not sent for?' he questioned. 'Come, deal justly with me; come, come, speak.'

A rising colour in their faces gave a look of guilt. So, he could detect the manipulations of his uncle and his mother in all this!

They hesitated, glanced at each other, and then back at him.

'My lord,' they admitted uneasily, 'we were sent for.'

'I will tell you why,' Hamlet said, bitterly. 'I have of late lost all my mirth, foregone all customs of exercise . . .'

He turned away as though quite suddenly he lost all interest that they were there. And then he looked at them again, and his gaze was harsh.

'What a piece of work is man! How noble in reason! In form and moving how express and admirable! In action how like an angel! In understanding how like a god!' He searched their faces for these glories, and despaired. Yet once he had seen this richness in his fellow men.

His companions laughed a little nervously. This truly was not the companion of their youth! But remembering their commission from the king, Rosencrantz told him about the actors on their way to Elsinore. It was a theatre company that Hamlet knew well.

Hamlet seemed to shake his gloom away. He grasped their hands again. 'You are welcome,' he said courteously. 'But,' he wagged a finger at them both, 'my uncle-father and aunt-mother are deceived.'

'In what?' asked Guildenstern.

'I am but mad north-north west,' said Hamlet, mockery gleaming in his eyes. 'When the wind is southerly I know a hawk from a hand-saw.'

And already the actors were entering the halls, with bows and flourishes and sparkling swirls of costume. Hamlet greeted old friends enthusiastically, noticing how each was taller, older, bearded, or not, since last they had met. 'Come, give us a taste of your quality,' he urged.'The rugged Pyrrhus, he whose sable arms . . .'

The actors took it up from him, unfolding a wild tale of vengeance and the sorrow of a widow, Hecuba, across the dead body of her husband . . . And Hamlet watched, enthralled, a whirlpool of warring thoughts erupting in his mind. On an impulse, as the actors turned to leave for rest and refreshment, he stopped one of them.

'Do you hear me, old friend,' he asked, 'can you play *The Murder of Gonzago*, and a speech of some dozen lines which I would insert in it?'

'Aye, my lord,' the actor agreed.

'We'll have it tomorrow night.' Hamlet watched him go. He felt his head was going to burst with the wild turbulence within!

'Oh what a rogue and peasant slave am I!' he almost wept. Was it not monstrous that this actor could, in a mere piece of fiction, a mere play, so work his passion up, that this whole face grew pale and tears welled in his eyes . . . what was Hecuba to him or he to Hecuba that he should weep for her? 'What would he do had he the motive for passion that I have? He would drown the stage with tears! Yet I can say nothing . . !' Two months ago the ghost had come to him. Two months! Two months had trickled past and there was nothing but a numbness in him whenever he thought of it.

'Am I a coward?' He searched in desperation for a reason for the heaviness which bound his heart and brain and stilled all movement towards revenge. Surely there could be no villain more deserving of a bloody death than Claudius! Bloody, bawdy villain! Remorseless, treacherous, lecherous, kindless villain!

His legs trembled as though the stream of words burned all their strength away. 'This is most brave,' he told himself sarcastically, 'that I, the son of a dear father murdered, prompted to my revenge by heaven and hell, must unpack my heart with words and fall to cursing!'

Everything called him to kill the villain and to draw his mother from the stinking nest in which she lay.

And yet he had not done it.

Each day entrenched the villain further in the wealth and power that he had seized by the murder of a king.

And yet he, Hamlet, had done nothing.

Once he had the glimmering of a plan: his madness had been a disguise to buy him time, from which he meant to come and take revenge. But now two months had gone and still it was not done.

Yet now, the gleam of something new . . . a thought he'd had, just as the actors left . . . The play!

111

'I'll have the actors play something like the murder of my father before my uncle,' he told himself. 'I'll observe his looks. If he but flinches, I know my course. The spirit that I have seen may be the devil, and the devil has power to assume a pleasing shape . . .'

But if he put the spirit's words to the test and proved it was no devil tempting him, perhaps this crippling numbness would lift and he could do what must be done. 'The play's the thing,' he told himself again, 'wherein I'll catch the conscience of the king.'

It seemed that Rosencrantz and Guildenstern could throw no light on Hamlet's madness. So now Ophelia was set to draw it out, and even the queen banished so that Claudius and Polonius could hide alone and watch Ophelia's encounter with the prince. The queen went willingly, thinking how simple and pleasant it would be if Ophelia were the cause of what so ailed her son, for then her virtues could be used to bring him to his usual self again!

Hurriedly Polonius pushed Ophelia into the hall. And so it was that the young girl found herself abandoned there, while Claudius and Polonius lurked behind a curtain and watched her every move. She was bewildered and uncertain of the part she was to play and yet she hoped with a kind of desperation that someone would at last confirm the cause of Hamlet's illness and find a cure for him.

Unknowing of the hidden watchers, or of Ophelia's shy figure in the shadows, Hamlet wandered by. The sudden certainties that had held him as he planned the play had faded, and a vast desolation welled in him again, as though he floated without substance through the world.

If only he could simply cease!

'To be or not to be, that is the question,' he told himself. 'To die; to sleep,' his mind sniffed after the thought as would a dog along a trail; 'To die, to sleep, perhaps to dream . . . Ay,' he nodded, 'there's the obstacle, for in that sleep of death what dreams may come!'

A flutter of movement caught his eye: he thrust the privacy of thought away, and turned.

'Good my lord,' Ophelia faltered, looking unwillingly into his face. 'How does your honour for this many a day?'

'I humbly thank you, well, well, well,' he answered, noticing the flare of colour in her face and the nervous glances which she threw about her. Once he had trusted this girl's soft innocence, and loved her well for it.

Now he watched her closely, wondering.

She offered some gifts that he had given her, and urged him to take them back.

'No, not I, I never gave you anything,' Hamlet dismissed them, and watched her closer still. She shrank from the harshness in his voice.

And still he watched her. What was she doing? Was she another trap for him, like Rosencrantz and Guildenstern? Was this frail beauty that he loved a thing of falseness, treachery and ugliness as was his mother?

He pulled the cloak of his madness about him and stared through its mask at her. 'Are you honest,' he asked sharply.

'My lord?' Ophelia enquired, in some confusion.

Then, as though a curtain lifted from his face, his eyes softened. 'I did love you once,' he murmured.

'Indeed, my lord, you made me believe so,' she said.

Believe! What was belief? He had believed that his mother so loved his father that she would die without his life to give her strength. 'You should not have believed me, I loved you not,' he turned from Ophelia, this girl who had become a thing of falseness like his mother.

'I was the more deceived,' faltered Ophelia.

A new suspicion leapt to his mind. 'Where's your father?'

The question whipped across Ophelia's shrinking heart. What would he do if he discovered that her father and the king lurked close?

'At home, my lord,' she whispered in shame, looking down.

'Let the doors be shut upon him that he may play the fool nowhere but in his own house. Farewell,' said Hamlet.

'Oh heavenly powers restore him!' Ophelia closed her eyes and felt that she would surely drown in the despair which swept over her. But suddenly his breath was hot against her face again, and opening her eyes she winced beneath a gaze of such contempt in Hamlet's face as she had never seen before. Could this embittered anger really be for her? She pushed him desperately away.

'I say we will have no more marriage! Those that are married already,' Hamlet turned and looked towards the curtain which shielded the secret watchers, 'all but one shall live.'

He looked back at her stricken face, as though a brief ray of warmth still tried to shine through the hatred in his words. But in a moment it was gone, and so was he.

Her last strength drained, Ophelia sank to the floor. She had once drunk the music of his vows of love! Yet here his noble mind, like sweet bells jangled, was out of tune and harsh.

Claudius swooped with Polonius from their spying place.

'Love!' scorned Claudius, 'His affections do not that way tend. Nor what he spoke, though it lacked form a little, it was not like madness.'

No, there was something else to this: all his instincts told him that there was more to this than Hamlet wanted them to know; and Claudius' ready sense of danger warned him that the menace was drawing nearer by the hour.

'He shall be sent with speed to England,' he told Polonius. Might not the sight of seas and other countries dispel his mood, he argued with the old councillor. At all costs, he knew, Prince Hamlet must be removed at once from Elsinore.

But Polonius was still certain that the prince was mad only for his daughter's love. Just one more scheme to test the matter out! This time the queen would be the bait. Let her entreat her son to show the causes of his grief: Polonius would be placed, of course, to hear their private conversation. And so another plot was hatched.

Hamlet also prepared his plan with care. He coached the actors how to speak the words he had written. And with a restless excitement he sought Horatio.

'There is a play tonight before the king,' he told him. 'One scene of it comes near the events which I have told you of my father's death. Observe my uncle. If his guilt does not reveal itself, it is an evil ghost that we have seen!'

Aghast at what he heard, Horatio agreed. At all costs this matter must, once and for all, be set to rights.

The time had come. They all came to watch the play: the king and queen, Polonius and Ophelia, Rosencrantz and Guildenstern and a hundred shining courtiers floating in with rustlings, and murmurings, and silken, painted smiles.

Hamlet greeted them all with witty jokes that danced a flippant jig about them, while the king thrust off his quips with an impatient look.

'Come here, my dear Hamlet, sit by me,' the queen said, trying to calm her excited son.

'No, good mother, here's metal more attractive,' he said, turning to Ophelia sitting with downcast eyes, her face a patchwork of misery.

'You are merry, my lord,' she answered Hamlet's bawdy humour, quietly, yet flinching inwardly with every word he spoke.

'What should a man do but be merry,' he answered with a laugh, 'for look you, how cheerfully my mother looks, and my father died within these two hours!'

'No,' said Ophelia, gently now, 'it is twice two months, my Lord.'

'So long!' said Hamlet. 'Oh heavens, die two months ago and not forgotten yet! Then there's hope a great man's memory may outlive his life half a year!'

But now the lights were dimmed, and music played. The murmurs of the shimmering audience died away, and king and queen began to smile expectantly.

Two actors came before them, dressed as a king and queen. They began an elegant mime: the queen showed her vast love for the king. The king lay down to sleep. The queen went out. At once a man crept in, and poured a deadly poison in the sleeping monarch's ear. The queen returned, wildly lamenting the king's death. The poisoner returned and joined her in her show of grief. The dead king's body was carried away. The poisoner began to woo the queen with gifts. At first unwilling, she at last accepted them.

The royal pair and all the gilded courtiers watched the mime. Hamlet and Horatio watched King Claudius. His smile had frozen on his face.

The mime had ended, and now the play began again, this time with words to tell the story. The player queen protested to the player king how she would love him for ever more and never wed again, should ever he lie dead.

'Madam, how do you like this play?' Hamlet asked his mother.

'The lady does protest too much, I think,' the queen answered comfortably.

'Aye, but she'll keep her word,' Hamlet assured her with a knowing smile.

Claudius smile was now a wound across his face that would not close.

The play continued. The poisoner came in, and bent across the sleeping king to pour the poison in his ear . . .

Hamlet could contain his wild excitement no longer. 'He poisons him in the garden for his crown. You shall see how the murderer gets the dead king's wife . . .'

The gash across Claudius' face opened to a roar.

'Give me some light!' he bellowed, and swept away, and with a crash of fallen chairs the courtiers scuttled in his wake.

'Did you perceive?' Hamlet asked Horatio. 'Upon the talk of poisoning?'

'Very well, my lord,' replied Horatio in horror. The king had truly fled before the sight of his own deeds!

But here came Rosencrantz and Guildenstern again, with royal messages for Hamlet: the king was angry and the queen demanded to see Hamlet in her room! Hamlet watched these old school friends delivering messages for king and queen. Their partnership with his corrupted mother and her damned husband had once made him a little sad, but now it angered him with searing pain. So many people playing games, circling about him like hunters round an animal in a trap!

And suddenly he seized a recorder from a passing actor and thrust the instrument at Guildenstern.

'Will you play upon this pipe?' he demanded.

'My lord, I cannot,' said Guildenstern, much startled.

116

'I beg you,' pressed Hamlet. 'It is as easy as lying. Look, these are the stops.'

'But I do not have the skill,' repeated Guildenstern.

'Why, look you now,' Hamlet challenged him angrily, 'you would play upon *me* as upon a pipe! You would seem to know *my* stops. You would sound *me* from the lowest note to the top. God, do you think I am easier to be played on than a pipe!'

He gestured them away, for he had done with friends like this.

He stood alone.

'It is now the very witching time of night,' he breathed. 'Now could I drink hot blood and do such bitter business as the day would quake to look upon.' He strove to calm his racing thoughts. Softly: now to his mother. But he must not hurt her. 'I will speak daggers to her, but use none,' he told himself.

The king was deep in conference with Rosencrantz and Guildenstern. Of one thing Claudius was certain: this play had been no casual accident. Hamlet was playing with him, and the scent of danger in Claudius' nostrils was sour.

'It is not safe to let his madness rage,' he argued. 'He shall go now to England along with you. Such dangers as are threatened by his lunacies should not be left to roam so close to the throne of Denmark . . .'

With only half an ear he heard Polonius say that Hamlet was going to his mother's room, to which Polonius would hurry, to hide and hear their conversation. Claudius had other matters on his mind. That play! How foul his acts had looked, grimacing at him from those mouths and eyes! For the first time he saw the deed as others would see it.

'Oh my offence is rank! It smells to heaven! A brother's murder!' Perhaps he should ask forgiveness from God? 'But what form of prayer can serve my turn? Forgive me my foul murder? That cannot be, since I still have those things for which I did the murder: my crown, my ambition and my queen. Can one be pardoned and still keep the things for which one sinned?'

Perhaps in a house of God he might find prayer easier. He entered the castle chapel. 'Oh wretched state! Help, angels!' He forced his knees to bend. Perhaps if he prayed here he would be safe . . .

And so he knelt. As he did the source of all his terrors came behind him. Hamlet saw the kneeling figure of his enemy and his broad back offered like a sacrifice to any ready sword, and quickly he drew his own.

'Now might I do it, pat. Now while he is praying.' The sword trembled as he raised it.

'And now I'll do it.' Still the weapon hovered and did not fall. 'And so he goes to heaven and so am I revenged?' The sword fell, unused, to his side, and despair filled him again. Kill Claudius while he prayed? No, that could not be. 'Kill him while he is drunk, or in the incestuous pleasures of his bed, that would be a fitting death for such a man . . .'

He backed away, sheathing his sword, and still arguing within himself. Kill, kill, revenge, the hammer drove on through his brain.

And somewhere beyond the circling arguments that he knew so well, there was the only rhythm that he really heard. His father was not revenged. He had not done it.

In her bedroom he faced the queen. 'Now, mother, what's the matter?'

'Hamlet, you have much offended your father,' his mother said, with unusual coldness in her tone.

'Mother, *you* have much offended my father,' Hamlet retorted.

She coloured, and her comfortable serenity was distorted by a look of unaccustomed anger.

'Have you forgotten who I am?' she demanded.

'No, not so. You are the queen, your husband's brother's wife: and, would it were not so, you are my mother.' He grasped her arm in sudden rage, 'You do not go,' he hissed, 'until I set up a mirror where you may see the inmost part of you.'

In sudden fear the queen drew back. 'Will you murder me? Help!'

Behind the curtain, the listening Polonius yelped.

'How now!' cried Hamlet, drawing his sword. 'A rat? Dead!' and fiercely he thrust his sword into the curtain.

'What have you done?' the queen gasped in disbelief.

'I do not know,' Hamlet cried, staring at the blood upon his sword. A wild hope had seized him, 'Is it the king?'

'Oh what a rash and bloody deed is this,' the queen was sobbing, knowing it was the wily councillor who had been killed.

'A bloody deed!' snorted Hamlet. 'Almost as bad, good mother, as kill a king and marry with his brother!'

The queen stared at him. As kill a king! She could not fathom what he meant.

118

Hamlet twitched back the curtain to see the body. Hope died in him. 'You wretched, rash, intruding fool, farewell,' he murmured. 'I took you for the king!' He let the curtain drop. 'Peace,' he hushed his mother. 'Sit you down, and let me wring your heart.'

'What have I done, that you dare wag your tongue in noise so rude against me?' pleaded the queen.

He lifted his father's portrait on a chain around his neck. 'Look here. This *was* your husband. Look you now what follows,' he seized the portrait of Claudius which stood by his mother's bed. 'Here *is* your husband: like a mildewed ear blasting his wholesome brother. Have you eyes? You cannot call it love!'

'Oh Hamlet, speak no more,' his mother begged. 'You turn my eyes into my very soul and there I see such black and grained spots . . .'

'But to live in the rank sweat of his bed, stewed in corruption, honeying and making love over the nasty sty like pigs . . .' Hamlet pleaded with her.

'These words like daggers enter my ears. No more, sweet Hamlet! No more,' she entreated him. 'You tear my heart in two!'

'Throw away the worser part of it and live the purer with the other half,' he urged her, gentler now. 'Go not to my uncle's bed.' He searched her face for signs of new-found strength and honesty.

'I must go to England, you know that?' he asked.

The queen sighed heavily. 'I had forgotten.'

'And my two schoolfellows, whom I will trust as I would trust fanged adders, will sweep me on my way.'

His mother watched him go, dragging the body of Polonius with him. Her love for him warred with a terror at the madness that she still suspected in her son's wild brain; and yet below it all there was a throbbing guilt that told her, in her innermost heart, that Prince Hamlet was not mad and spoke only the truth.

The news of Polonius' death pierced through the king like a swordthrust to his heart: how close the danger came to him! Had he been hiding with Polonius, Hamlet's sword would have been for him.

Hamlet must be got to England with all possible speed! The preparations had been carefully made: Hamlet was now a prisoner, and in the hands of Rosencrantz and Guildenstern, Claudius had entrusted letters, sealed and directed to the King of England.

In these letters Claudius asked that, on arrival on England's shores, Hamlet should be instantly put to death.

Hamlet, close guarded by Rosencrantz and Guildenstern, travelled towards his ship, and death, in England. And so it came about that he stood high up on a hill, and looked down over the army of Prince Fortinbras of Norway as it moved across the plains of Denmark, bound for war in Poland.

Everything he saw told him of others' speed, and strength, and will to act! Here were these twenty thousand men marching to war, led on by a prince of steel who did not flinch from the task before him!

'I do not know why yet I live to say "this thing's to be done,"' Hamlet ached with shame, self-loathing and disgust. 'I have cause and will and strength and means to do it. How stand I then? I that have a father killed, a mother stained, excitements of my reason and my blood . . . And yet I let all sleep.'

'Oh from this time forth,' he told himself for perhaps the hundredth time, 'my thoughts be bloody or be nothing worth!'

The fragile Ophelia was floundering in the evil mire of Elsinore, and knew that she was drowning. So fast the blows beat down on her! Severed from Hamlet by her father's hand, bewildered by the plots and counterplots in which she was pushed and pulled, savaged by the bitter mistrust in Hamlet's scorn of her, her misery had stretched to breaking point. And now her father was dead, killed by the man she loved.

Her fragile nature snapped, like a sweet flower-laden branch caught in a storm, its blossoms torn and trampled on the ground, its strength stripped bare. Whispering strange snatches of half-heard bawdy tavern songs, she wandered lonely in the castle halls; with knowing nods and winks she told of tricks and plots, grew angry, sorrowful, sighed, laughed, and roamed on, always, always alone . . .

The courtiers whispered of her tragedy. They whispered too about her brother, for Laertes had learned of his father's death and had returned, hot-foot from France.

Claudius prepared carefully. Steadily he turned Laertes' rage towards the prince. The wasted figure of Ophelia drifted by, no recognition of her brother on her face, only a scrap of song upon her lips and arms laden with imagined gifts of flowers which she bestowed with gentle grace on everyone she saw. And all the while she sang of violets withering when her father died, of death and tombs and graves.

Claudius watched Laertes, and saw him burning now with far more than rage at his father's death, for here also were a sister's wasted wits to be revenged! Claudius was swift to give a thousand reasons why he had not moved against Prince Hamlet openly: the queen so loved her son; the people loved him too and would not easily accept the sight of him accused of murder.

He did not give the most important reason of all, that he feared what Hamlet, on trial, might say about the murder of a king!

Then came the news that spiked their musings into daggers and awoke old terrors in Claudius . . . Hamlet was not on board the ship approaching England and his death! He was again in Denmark.

At once Claudius sharpened his ready wits to cunning. 'What would you undertake against this murderer to show yourself your father's son in deed more than in words?' he asked Laertes.

The young man's face flamed with a rush of vicious anger. 'To cut his throat in the church!'

Here was the man to kill the prince! It must be done, thought Claudius, in such a way that everyone would think it was an accident. Laertes was so much a son of his old wily father that he saw no dishonour in the catching of their prey by devious means and hidden murder. The plot was laid: a fencing match between Hamlet and Laertes – a swordfight for sport to match their skills against each other. Hamlet, Claudius assured Laertes, was too trusting a man to check the weapons. He would not know that Laertes used a blade without a button to cover its deadly point. Nor would he know that Laertes' blade was poisoned, so that the slightest scratch would bring an instant death to Hamlet. Nor that the king would have ready a poisoned cup . . . *This* time there would be no escape from death for Hamlet.

There was a churchyard close beside the towers of Elsinore, and here two gravediggers dug a grave. Here, the poor battered frame of frail Ophelia would be laid, at last, to rest.

Clambering to hang garlands of wild flowers on the weeping branches of a willow tree, she had fallen to the brook below, and floated there, cushioned on her billowing skirts, chanting wistful snatches of old tunes, until her sodden garments pulled her to her muddy, lonely death. So had Ophelia finally escaped the mire of Elsinore.

Being much used to the grim task of making holes for dead people to lie in, the gravediggers chattered and joked about their work as would any workman wiling away a long and weary day. 'Who builds stronger than a mason, a shipwright or a carpenter?' one challenged the other.

'A gravemaker,' came the answer, with a snort of mirth, 'for the house that he makes lasts till Doomsday!'

The other tittered at this ready wit, and in this jovial mood they little noticed the two men who came upon their merriment and watched them curiously. Horatio and Hamlet were on their way from seashore to Elsinore, Hamlet telling all that had happened since he set sail.

What a turn of fate there had been! From the moment he had boarded that fateful ship some instinct had told him that there was a particular new devilry afoot. Secretly, by night, he had obtained the letters carried by Rosencrantz and Guildenstern, and in them he had read of Claudius' order for his death in England. No sooner had he found this out than they had been attacked by pirates, and Hamlet, leaping aboard the pirate ship, was taken prisoner, while his own ship broke free and swept on its way to England. And Rosencrantz and Guildenstern, these messengers of death, now carried letters, written and sealed by Hamlet, requesting that the bearers of the letters be put to instant death!

'So Guildenstern and Rosencrantz go to it,' Horatio murmured, with awestruck horror at their fate.

'Why, they did make love to this employment!' Hamlet swept his misgivings aside. 'They are not near my conscience.' But the pirates had been honourable, and had dealt fairly with him. They had come to an agreement to put him down on Denmark's shores.

And so back to Elsinore, and to his uncle. But now the self-disgust with which he'd viewed the massing armies of Prince Fortinbras had been fed by the strange events at sea to a kind of recklessness, a drive to return and ride the current of fate wherever it carried him . . .

Yet this jovial show of wit over the digging of a grave made him grow cold again. Could death become so common-place? These skulls that peeped so desolately from the earth were treated here as little more than lumps of earth! Yet once they had tongues to sing and brains to think . . . He shuddered, lifting up a skull and staring into its sightless gaze, 'Do you think Alexander the Great looked like this in the earth?' he asked Horatio. 'Alexander died, Alexander was buried, Alexander returns to dust,' he mused.

'Imperious Caesar, dead and turned to clay,
Might stop a hole to keep the wind away.'

Horatio put a quieting hand upon his arm: a train of mourners was
drawing near, bearing the body of a girl.

Hamlet looked up, and stopped then in disbelief. 'The fair Ophelia!'
he whispered. A flame shot through him, a memory of almost buried
love, a look of her as he had seen her last . . .

'Sweets to the sweet: farewell!' the mournful tones of his mother
reached his ears. She scattered flowers across Ophelia's body. 'I hoped
you would have been my Hamlet's wife.'

Unshed tears pricked behind Hamlet's eyes, the crowding misery of
guilt, the sudden understanding of how wrongly he had savaged her.
He saw Laertes leap into the grave and take his sister's body in his arms.
How dare they mouth of sorrows, grief and loss, these kings and queens
and courtiers who used people as toys, as playthings for their needs! He
charged blindly forwards, and with a cry of 'This is I, Hamlet the
Dane,' he leapt into the grave, defying one and all to match his anguish.

'The devil take your soul,' Laertes yelled, and flew at him.

'Pluck them apart,' bellowed the king. The two were hauled out from
the grave, and Hamlet faced Laertes.

'I loved Ophelia!' he cried. 'Forty thousand brothers could not with
all their quantity of love make up my sum. Will you weep? Will you
fight? Will you eat crocodile? I'll do it! Do you come here to outface me
with leaping in her grave? Be buried now with her and so will I!'

King Claudius watched them both with narrowed eyes. Now quickly
to this fencing match: no delays. Only a fight to Hamlet's certain death
would suit his purposes.

Hamlet had calmed. In quieter mood he reflected on Laertes' bitter
rage, and how the world had dealt sore blows to this young man. A
father killed (and by his, Hamlet's hand), a sister maddened and dead:
it seemed to Hamlet now that it was the mirror portrait of his own
misery, and he regretted his own anger in the grave.

So he accepted the fencing match suggested by the king to settle the
hot blood between him and Laertes in honourable fashion.

For a moment a shifting unease moved deep within him, like a
stirring from the rottenness of Elsinore. But then he pushed it aside.
'If your mind dislikes anything, obey it,' Horatio pressed him. 'I will

123

say you are not well.'

'Not a whit!' said Hamlet. 'There's special fate in the fall of a sparrow. If it is now, it is not to come. If it is not to come, it will be now. If it is not now, yet it will come: the readiness is all!'

The time had come. The courtiers came to watch the fencing match.

'Give me your pardon, sir; I have done you wrong,' Prince Hamlet said to Polonius' son.

Laertes seemed to receive the apology courteously enough, but still insisted that they satisfy their honour with the match.

Hamlet gestured towards the weapons, 'give us the swords.'

'This is too heavy,' Laertes said, 'let me see another.' He picked up the unprotected, poisoned blade.

'Are they all the same length?' asked Hamlet, and chose one casually, making passes through the air with it to feel its weight and balance.

King Claudius called for wine. 'The king drinks to Hamlet,' he said, and held the cup aloft. 'And in the cup I will throw this pearl . . .' Claudius held up his master-stroke, the pearl of secret poison.

The fencing bout began. Hamlet and Laertes circled warily, their weapons nosing out the other's speed and skill with thrust and counter-thrust, with rapid feints and parries.

And then with cat-like leap and whip-like blade, Hamlet lunged and caught Laertes.

'A hit,' the cry rose from the courtiers.

The king dropped the pearl of death into the cup. 'Give him the cup,' he ordered with a benevolent smile.

'I'll play this bout first,' said Hamlet.

The second bout began. 'Another hit, what say you?' Hamlet panted.

'A touch, a touch, I do confess,' Laertes said. He seemed, the audience noticed, to be holding back, as though he waited for a moment yet to come.

'Here Hamlet, take my napkin and rub your brow,' the queen said. 'The queen drinks to your fortune, Hamlet.' She lifted the poisoned cup.

'Do not drink!' the king rose to his feet in shock.

'I will, my lord,' the queen smiled at him, playfully defiant, and raised the poisoned cup. She took a long, luxurious drink from it.

Claudius sank to his seat. 'It is too late!' And in a dream of horror he saw Laertes' poisoned blade dart out and pierce the prince's side. He saw the prince stare down at trickling blood . . .

A sudden understanding flared in Hamlet. This was no sport! This was a fight for life! With a great yell of fury he leapt at Laertes, and in the scuffling wrestled the poisoned blade away and with the weapon in his hands, he pierced the arm of Polonius' treacherous son.

The queen stood up, half-staggered towards her son, and fell.

Hamlet swayed, suddenly. A lightness had ovecome his limbs. 'How is the queen?' he panted.

'She faints to see them bleed,' Claudius croaked in panic.

'No, no, the drink. Oh my dear Hamlet, I am poisoned,' the queen cried, and fell back, dead.

'Villainy!' cried Hamlet. 'Let the door be locked! Treachery, seek it out!'

'It is here, Hamlet; Hamlet you are killed.' Laertes raised himself in twisting agony, and pointed to the poisoned sword. From lips already paling in death, he poured out the tale of treachery.

Hamlet held Laertes' sword. He looked at the king. Claudius understood, and rose in terror. The drumming in Hamlet's brain reached a crescendo, and with a shout of pent-up rage and hate he rushed at the shrinking figure of the king and thrust the blade deep into him. 'Here you incestuous, murderous, damned Dane. Drink your potion! Follow my mother!' and he forced the poisoned cup between the trembling lips.

He stumbled back into Horatio's arms. A vast void was swallowing him, and he sank deep into it. The sound of marching feet rang through the castle halls. 'What warlike noise is this?' he breathed; struggling to lift his head. It was young Fortinbras, the prince of steel, returning from his wars in Poland and coming to Elsinore, victorious.

Hamlet fell back, and closed his eyes. 'I die, Horatio,' his voice writhed in agony. 'The potent poison overwhelms my spirit. But I do prophesy the throne of Denmark will fall on Fortinbras. He has my dying vote: so tell him.' He sighed a deep shuddering sigh. 'The rest is silence.'

Horatio held the crumpled body of his friend. 'Now cracks a noble heart,' he whispered. 'Good night, sweet prince, and flights of angels sing you to your rest.'

And so Prince Fortinbras came upon the havoc of death which

strewed the halls of Elsinore and stood in awe before the desolate sight.
A king, a queen, a prince, a courtier all dead. Here was a tale to chill the
marrow of the bravest soldier's bones! He stood in silence above the
Prince of Denmark's body, and heard the tragic story from the loyal
Horatio's lips.

Then he raised his head and looked around the devastation that was
Elsinore. 'Let four captains bear Hamlet, like a soldier, to the stage,' he
said. 'Let the soldiers' music and the rites of war speak loudly for him!
He was likely, had he lived, to have proved most royal . . .'